BORN AGAIN, DEAD AGAIN

BORN AGAIN, DEAD AGAIN

This book is about spiritual warfare within oneself

SERGIO LOVETT

Library of Congress Control Number:		2012913686
ISBN:	Hardcover	978-1-4771-5183-9
	Softcover	978-1-4771-5182-2
	Ebook	978-1-4771-5184-6

This book was printed in the United States of America.

To order additional copies of this book, contact:
Xlibris Corporation
1-888-795-4274
www.Xlibris.com
Orders@Xlibris.com
119456

DEDICATION

This book is dedicated to God and my children: as a memoir of my life.

Tavares

Good morning, Jesus, today is July 19, 1967. I am seven years old today. I wonder if I'm going to get a birthday present today, or will it be just like any other day here in Tavares, Florida? Extremely hot and with nothing to do, if the heat and gnats don't kill you by day, then surely the mosquitoes will kill you by night.

The mosquitoes are so bad here that the city has a fleet of trucks that rides around at night and spray chemicals in the air to kill them. Most of my friends and I like to run behind the truck in the mist of the spray. I guess the mosquitoes are so bad because of all the lakes around here. There's a body of water everywhere I go.

I hope my dad takes me out on the boat to go fishing today; that's my most favorite thing to do. It is also the only chance I get to spend some quality time with my dad without him hollering at me about something. Actually, the only time he says anything to me is right before and during one of his ass whippings.

I'm not talking about a mere spanking; no, I'm talking about feeling it for three days after the fact ass whipping. I have three brothers, and they never get whipped quite as bad as I do. My mom has to stop him because she's afraid he's going to hurt me. She always goes running to save me, screaming, "Roy, Roy, Roy, please stop hitting that boy before you hurt him!"

She can scream all she wants, but he's not going to stop beating me until he knows I'm physically and emotionally hurt. I'm afraid of my dad because he's a very mean man. He never smiles or laughs, he never plays with me, and he never talks to me. He only shouts at me when he wants me to do something for him.

Most likely I won't be going fishing on my birthday because he's in a bad mood. I can hear him now fussing at my mom about something. Lady, our

German shepherd, is starting to get agitated. She's actually growling and has both of her ears straight up on the top of her head.

Lady and I are on the carport, so I'm trying to calm her down before my dad hears her. She's a very good dog, but she does not like my dad raising his voice at my mom. Uh-oh, here he comes, and Lady is still growling at him. Calm down, girl. It's going to be all right. "I know damn well you're not growling at me," my dad says. He makes a beeline right back into the house to his bedroom.

Here he comes again, but this time he has a shotgun in his hand. "Stop holding that dog and get the fuck out of the way," he says. "No, Dad, don't shoot her. She didn't mean it." He lifts the shotgun and says, "Boy, didn't I tell you to get the fuck out of the way? Now move." Scared, shaking, and crying, I reluctantly let her go and slowly back away.

Before I can say another word, *boom, boom!* Two shots ring out. It's a double-barrel shotgun, and he uses both shots. She's on the ground, bleeding and gasping for air. I run to her and pick her head up as she looks into my eyes and dies right in my arms. I have blood all over me from holding her, and I can't believe what just happened.

My mom runs out the door, screaming when she sees the blood all over me. Fortunately, I'm not hurt, but I can't say the same for Lady; she's dead. Mom takes me in the house to get me cleaned up, as my dad goes in the backyard to dig a shallow grave. He looks as if it doesn't bother him at all that he just killed the dog. He's only more pissed off now because he has to dig a hole.

A couple of days pass and I'm still afraid to look up at him while sitting at the dinner table. He hasn't said a word to me about killing Lady. It's as if nothing ever happened. None of us would dare question him, unless we wanted a beat down. All of us are afraid of him. When he says "Take out the garbage," we all jump up because we don't know whom he's talking to.

It is Wednesday, my favorite day of the week, and here comes the reason why: the Bible-study lady. She goes in her bus once a week and teaches all the kids in the neighborhood about Jesus. I love Jesus, and I'm the smartest student in her class. No one ever beats me to that bus door. "You sure are hungry for Jesus Christ," she says to me. "Yes, ma'am," I reply, "I love these stories."

The Bible-class lady has no idea that I have to call on Jesus every day or night. I have this big problem with the devil attacking me, when I dream and sometimes when I'm awake. The only way I can get rid of him is when I call on Jesus. Sometimes while I'm lying on the floor in the living room, watching television, the television will start moving farther and farther away from me, as if I were in a tunnel.

When it happens, everyone in the room seems to be suspended in time, my brothers, my sister, and my parents. Now here comes the devil, and he's the scariest thing I've ever seen. There's slobber dripping from the corner of his mouth while he laughs at me.

The devil then jumps on my back and pins me to the floor. I'm literally paralyzed. He puts both of his hands around my mouth and nose so that I can't scream or breathe. Then the jumping up and down on my back starts. He rides me like he's riding a wild horse. The only things I can move are my eyes, so I look to and fro around the room, and no one realizes what's going on.

Jesus, Jesus, Jesus, please help me, I cry out with my heart. I can't breathe, and he's going to kill me. Right before I feel that it's all over and I'm dead, finally he releases me and vanishes. I immediately look at my mom with tears in my eyes and ask, "Didn't you see that devil on my back?" She looks at me as if I were crazy and says, "Boy, you need to stop eating so much sugar."

She never believes my dreams when I tell them to her; in fact, no one does except my brother Ronald. The only reason he believes me is because he experienced an episode with me. A couple of weeks ago, I told him about the devil coming in the room at night when the rest of them are asleep.

The four of us sleep in the same room with a set of bunk beds, so we came up with a plan. I tied a piece of thread around my wrist, and it went across the room to his wrist. Surely enough after they fell asleep, I can hear the devil coming down the hallway. One of his feet drags slowly behind the other as he scrapes his fingernails across the wall. I can even hear the slobber drop out of his mouth to the floor, as if it were amplified a hundred times.

As he sticks his head in the door, I pull on the thread to awaken my brother Ronald. He sees what I see and jumps out of the bed, swinging fists and throwing elbows. All of a sudden, the commotion stops. I look at him with tears in my eyes and say, "See, I told you." We both get back in bed and not speak about what just happened.

Morning arrives and we're asleep when Dad opens the door and says, "Get up, get up out of that bed." He reaches down on the floor and picks up a rotten long tooth. He looks at it and asks us, "Which one of you brought this nasty animal tooth in the house?" We all look at him and say, "I didn't do it, Dad." I look over at my brother Ronald, and even he doesn't realize that it came from the devil's mouth last night.

A couple of weeks have passed by, and I haven't seen the devil in the house lately, but I'm sure he'll be back. My grandmother told me that I was born with a gift and the devil wants me to use it for his purpose, so that's the reason behind all the attacks. She says, "Baby, the Lord has got an important job for you to do, but the devil is going to try and stop you."

My grandmother is the best role model that I know. She's always singing to the Lord. I have never heard her use profanity in her conversations, nor have I ever seen her angry. She's always in good spirit, and I spend a lot of time around her. In fact, I like being at her house; it's like being on holy ground. The devil never attacks me while I'm there.

I'm bored because it's early in the morning and no one is outside in the street yet. My dad has a manual lawn mower that I can play with, so I'll go and cut some grass. I'm tired of pushing this thing, so I decide to spin the blade by hand and stick the grass in it. This is fun because the blades are sharp like razors. They slice one single strand of grass with no problem.

All of a sudden, I feel something wet splash across my face, I lick my lips, and it's the taste of blood. Oh my god, my finger is cut through the bone; it's dangling on by a mere piece of skin. The blades cut it so fast that I didn't feel it. I put my other hand up under the dangling finger just to keep it from falling all the way off. Now the blood is everywhere; it's coming out so fast.

I run into the house, screaming for my mom to help me. She immediately wraps up my entire hand to stop the bleeding. Now I'm in serious pain. I'm screaming and crying for help. The wrap has turned completely red, so she has to wrap another one on top. She's screaming, "Roy, Roy, this boy done cut his finger off." Dad storms in the room and says, "Boy, what the hell have you done?"

I tell him how it happened, and he grabs the belt and beats me so bad that I'm running and diving under tables to get away from him. My mom is screaming at him, "Roy, Roy, please stop beating him and take him to the doctor!" This time, she actually pulls him away from me and takes me to the doctor.

The hospital is too far away, so we go in town to see Dr. Bogus. His office is on Main Street in Tavares. There's a sign in front of the building that says Colored, with an arrow pointing toward the back of the building. Only white people can use the front door. We have to go all the way around the back in order to get in. Once we get inside, there's a thick glass wall between the black patients and the white patients.

My mom and I sit in the lobby while they attend to white patient after white patient. I know that we have been sitting here for an hour at least, and they didn't give me anything for pain yet. I'm about to scream, then finally, Lovett, the nurse, calls out. She takes me to the back, and I finally get a shot for the pain. The doctor stitched my finger back together and put it in a splint.

I'm right-handed, and my finger is cut from the right hand, so I have to learn how to do everything with my left hand. Writing, eating, picking things up are all difficult tasks now. My brothers tease me because Mom will not allow me to go outside and play anymore until I'm healed. That's fine with me because now they have to do all the work around the house without me.

Finally after months of recovering, I'm allowed to go outside and play again.

The first place I go to is next door. Someone is building a brand-new house there, and it is unfinished, which makes it an ideal place to play. When I walk inside, I hear funny noises, sexual noises coming from one of the bedrooms. I tiptoe quietly toward the room and peek inside. Oh shit, my brother is on top of a girl, hunching with no clothing on.

"Both of you are going to get a whipping because I'm going to tell Mom." My brother says, "Hold up, wait, do you want some of her?" I look at her long yellow legs wet from perspiration, and then I look into her eyes, and she says, "Come on and get on top of me, Sergio. I will show you what to do." I did as she said, and it was very exciting for me.

Well, what do you know, I just got my first piece of ass, and she is six years older than me. Surely I can't tell because I did the same thing as my brother did. If my mom finds out, she will tell my dad and he will whip the brakes off me. So I guess this will remain a secret between me and my brother.

There is a church behind our house, and it is so close that I can throw a rock and hit it. We go to another church up the street, and when the preacher is talking, I can't understand a word he's saying. I always get sleepy when I'm there because it seems so boring. The church behind the house is sanctified, and I can hear them shouting and dancing. I really want to go inside and play the drums that I hear.

My mom makes me go to her church every Sunday, and I sing in the choir. They make me lead the song "Trouble in My Way." I don't like singing in that church because every song is so slow and sad. So every Sunday I ask her, "Can I go to church behind the house?"

Finally after months of my asking and waiting, my mom agrees to let me go to the church behind the house. I stop at the front door of the church and just listen to the music; it sounds like they are having a Holy Ghost party inside. As soon as I step inside, the Holy Ghost jumps on me, and I'm shaking, crying, calling on the Lord.

The preacher asks if there is anyone that would like to dedicate their life to Christ. I immediately stand up and walk to him. He tells the entire church to pray over me while I continually call out the name Jesus. In doing so, I notice some type of white foamlike substance coming from my mouth, and the preacher says I'm purifying myself of past sins.

After everyone finished praying over me and I couldn't call on Jesus anymore because my voice was gone, the preacher stood me up off my knees. He puts his hand on my forehead and says, "Son, you are now born again. You are a child of God. Welcome to the family." I feel different inside, as if something just invaded my body, and I'm happy about being saved.

Months pass and I've been going to the church every Sunday. They even let me play the drums now. The devil must be upset with me about going to church and praising God, because he has started to attack me in my dreams. I stay up as long as I can because I'm afraid of what I'm going to see when I fall asleep. The dreams seem real, and I'm taken away by the depths of them.

Sometimes when I dream, I see myself in close-to-death situations, but right at the moment when I'm supposed to die, I always wake up. I talked to my grandmother about these dreams, and she told me that if I ever see myself die, I would surely be dead. That really scares me because I have dreams like that all the time.

Years pass by and I'm still experiencing the same type of dreams or, should I say, visions, because some of the things I see in my dreams seem to come to pass in reality. I'm still saved, and every day is a challenge trying to walk with God. I haven't said a curse word or done anything I consider bad since I've been born again.

Today my parents have company at the house, attending a small, private party. They are really having themselves a good time. The music is turned up so loud that you can actually hear it a block away as they dance like kids on sugar diets. The barbecue pork ribs that are on the grill are smoking up the entire neighborhood with a sweet aroma. The drinks are flowing, and money is being won and lost at the card table.

They all seem to be happy, without a problem to worry about. No one has started any trouble, even though they're all a little intoxicated. My mom rarely drinks alcoholic beverages, so she's about the only adult here that is not tipsy. "Roy, Roy, the telephone is for you," she shouts loudly to be heard over the music. Dad gets up and goes in the house to the phone, and when he comes back out, he doesn't look happy.

"Damn," he says, "I have to leave and go to a service call." My dad brings this huge company truck home that is designed for changing tires on big tractors and trailers. He works for BFGoodrich, and on Saturdays he is on call. My mom's sister Aunt Sadie's husband, Frank Neal, volunteers to ride with my dad on the service call. "I'll be back in about two hours," my dad says.

They load up in the big service truck and leave out, heading to the service call. The party continues and everyone is still having a good time. All of a sudden, my mom runs out of the house, crying and screaming, "Sadie, Sadie, Sadie, Lord have mercy, Sadie!"

"What's wrong, Louise? What's wrong?" my aunt Sadie says. "Calm down and tell me what in the world is going on."

Mom grabs her by both of her hands, looks into her eyes, and says, "Roy and Frank just had a very bad accident, and Frank is dead. He was thrown out of the truck on impact. Then the truck rolled over on top of him." They both start screaming and crying while embracing each other tightly, falling to their knees.

Seeing my mother and Aunt Sadie break down like that is immediately absorbed by me. I run to both of them, crying as well, and grab their necks. As I hold on to both of them, the Holy Ghost inside me is taking over my body. At this moment I have no control over my emotions or actions. The music stops, and everyone is silent for a few seconds that seem like an eternity.

I look into both of their eyes, and I can feel the pain that they are expressing to each other. The news of Frank's death has stunned us all; most of the guests at the party are crying and holding one another. "Mom, Mom," I cry out, "what about dad? Is he dead too?"

"No, son, your dad is in the hospital and he's going to be all right," she replies. I say softly and under my breath, "Thank you, Jesus."

I look over at the card table and the chair that Frank was sitting in, just thirty minutes ago. His drink was still sitting on the table, and I say to myself, "He was sitting right there, laughing, drinking, talking shit, and playing cards. How can this be, Lord?" My mom, Aunt Sadie, and a few others get in cars and take off to the hospital.

As I prepare for bed, I decide to try something weird that I overheard some elderly people speak about. Tonight I'm going to get in touch with the dead, Frank Neal, to be specific. I write a letter to him and put it on the side of my bed, along with a glass of water. I'm scared to death, but I'm curious enough to see this through, so I slowly drift off into sleep.

As I sleep and start dreaming about me being able to fly over people, my intuition takes over and I'm awake. It's Frank Neal, and he is in the house, coming down the hallway, straight for me. Oh shit, the door is opening and I can hear it squeaking. Immediately I roll over as if I'm asleep and pull the covers over my head. He's standing right next to my bed, but I'm afraid to look at him.

He has on a red pullover shirt with khaki pants, and I can hear the potato chip bag crumbling in his hand as he approaches the bed. It's my favorite snack, and he knows that. I can see the yellow bag even in the dark, Lay's Potato Chips. That is still not enough to get me to turn over and face him. I'm wondering if would he look the way he looked after the crash or not. I don't want to find out right now; all I want is for him to go away, and he does.

After a mostly sleepless night, morning finally arrives and I couldn't be happier to see daylight. Thank you, Jesus, for getting me through the night and waking me up this morning. I promise that I will never try to speak with the dead again.

My dad only has a minor injury to his knee from the accident, and he is back at work now. It's amazing that he didn't receive severe injuries from the impact. I saw a picture of the scene of the accident and read the newspaper article. The car was traveling on the wrong side of the road at a speed in excess of a hundred miles per hour. The truck is so big that the car went underneath it and flipped it over.

My dad pulls up from work just as we're starting to play football against a team of guys from uptown. They like to come out here in the country and get their ass kicked in a roughneck game, with no rules. We literally try to take each other's head off when we tackle. My brother throws me a long touchdown pass and I get hit hard anyway for scoring, even though I'm in the end zone.

As I stand up, I can feel a tingling sensation in my lower right leg. I look down at my leg, and oh shit, I have a cut so deep that all I see is white meat. I run into the house, and as soon as I see my dad, I start crying from fear of the ass whipping I'm about to get. The blood starts pouring from my leg as I stand before him. "Boy, didn't I tell you not to play around that broken glass? Come here," he says to me. Before I can answer him, my mom takes me in her arms, wraps the wound with gauze, and rushes me to the hospital.

Here I am again, stuck in the house; they won't allow me to go outside and play. My parents are at work; Donnie, my brother, who is four years older than I, is the only one in the house with me. Our cousin Charles, who is my aunt Sadie's son, comes in the door with a big brown paper sack and puts it on the table.

"Cousin, cousin," he says, calling for my brother Donnie, "come and help me bag this up." He dumps the contents of the paper sack onto the kitchen table, and it looks like a bunch of green leaves and twigs. "Man, you better get that garbage off of my mom's kitchen table, fool." He says, "This is not garbage, you idiot. This is marijuana, a whole pound of it. So if you keep your little mouth shut, I just might give you some of it."

"In school my teacher showed us films about how people act when they are high on drugs, and I don't want to jump off of a mountain or burn my hand with fire," I say to him. They both start laughing at me and say, "That's not going to happen if you smoke a little pot. It's only going to give you the munchies and have you laughing at shit. I'll roll one up and let you smoke it, and I guarantee you that you're not going to jump off of anything."

Charles passes me this superfat joint and says, "Go outside and smoke half of it, cousin." So I go in the backyard all alone, and I fire it up. Wow, this stuff is strong; I'm coughing up the cold in my chest. I'm starting to feel the effects of the pot in my head now, and I actually like this feeling.

I walk back into the house, and I say to Charles, "You're right. I'm definitely not going to jump off of anything." They both look at each other, and Charles says to Donnie, "He's handling it pretty well to be such a youngster."

"Do the Joker, do the Joker," Charles says to me. "I love to see you do that shit, man. It is so funny." He's referring to the character in *Batman*. Joker is the menacing goon. Everybody likes Batman on that show, but my favorite character is the Joker. I have all his moves and even his voice down pat. I can imitate him so well that Charles pays me money to entertain his dates. I'm high right now, so I guess I can give him a free show.

I surprise them this time; instead of doing the Joker, I do the Penguin. Charles and Donnie are crying with laughter. "When did you learn how to do that shit? It's funnier than the Joker," Charles says. "I've been working on it for a couple of weeks," I reply. "I thought that right now would be a good time to try it out." After showing off, I realized what I had just done. I'm not born again; I just smoked pot. I feel as if I just disappointed the Lord, so I guess now I'm dead again.

Months pass and I haven't had any weed to smoke on my own, but every now and then, Charles will sneak me a joint. School has been back in session only two months, and things are a lot different this year because they no longer have the races segregated from each other. We all go to the same school, black kids and white kids.

There's this one big white boy that's trying to bully me around, and I persistently try to ignore him, but he's making that difficult. He always seems to show up when I'm talking to girls, especially white girls. I think the fact that they are attracted to me really disturbs him.

It is recess time, and we all go out to the playground to play tag football. As the game progresses, the white boy who is on the other team keeps giving me the evil eye. After the ball is snapped, he heads straight toward me and knocks me down then calls me a fucking nigger.

I look at him right in the eyes, as I get up and dust off the dirt from my clothing. Then without warning, I grab both of his legs, pick him up, and slam him down to the ground. Once he's on the ground, I stomp on him until the teacher pulls me away. "Sergio, Sergio, what are you doing? Stop it right now," she says. I tell her that he's the one that started the fight, and she still sends me to the principal's office.

The principal sits me down and tells me how bad I am for fighting regardless of what initiated it. Then he pulls out this huge paddle, with holes in it, and tells me to bend over his desk. I look up at this big white man and say, "You better call my daddy because you are not going to hit me with that paddle." He grabs me by my arm, I snatch it away from him and shout, "Call my daddy!"

"All right, young man," he says, "I'll do just that. Take a seat up front." My dad arrives from his job about thirty minutes later, and I'm scared because he looks pissed off to be distracted from his work. He listens to every word carefully as the principal tells him his version of the events. Then he turns to me and asks me what happened; surprisingly he agrees with me. He tells the principal that no one is allowed to spank his kids because he can handle that himself. I say quietly to myself, "I know that's right because he'll beat the brakes off of you."

Dad takes me home, and I can't believe that I'm not getting a whipping. I'm waiting for him to pull off his belt, but he doesn't. The only thing he says to me is "Don't go back out of the house today." My dad is a trip; he never speaks a lot of words to me. His way of showing love is buying us things that the other kids don't have, like minibikes and go-carts. He also makes sure that the bills are paid, we never lack anything, so I'll give him his credit for that.

Every Friday and Saturday early evening, when Dad comes home from work, he takes a shower and hits the streets. When he leaves, he is always dressed to kill and smelling good. My mom knows that he is cheating, but I never hear her complain about it. It is like a normal routine; he is never anywhere to be found on those nights.

Years have passed and it is 1972; school has been back in session for only a couple of months. Nothing in Tavares has changed except that the white folks finally took down the signs that they had all over town. They had signs on the public bathrooms and water fountains that said White Only. There were also signs that said Colored People, with an arrow to point us to the back entrances of business establishments.

Even though the signs are gone, the mentality remains the same. They literally have KKK rallies less than two miles of where we live, and the town is still very much segregated.

My younger brother Rob and I are waiting for my mom to pick us up from Grandma's house, and she's late. Her being late is extremely unusual; that is something that has never happened before. "Sergio, Sergio, here she comes," Rob says, as the car approaches from down the street. The car stops in front of us, and I immediately feel that something is wrong, because my mom is not inside the car. Donnie my other brother, is here to pick us up.

"Where is Mom, Donnie? Where is Mom?" I ask him in a frantic way as I stare him straight in the eyes. He looks at Rob before he looks at me and says, "Mom is gone, and she will not be coming back here to stay, ever again."

"What do you mean she's gone?" I reply. "Gone where? She can't just leave us here with Dad all by ourselves." Donnie says, "Calm down, Sergio. Everything is going to be all right."

So I take a deep breath and prepare myself for the unknown, as Donnie begins to speak slowly. "I took Mom to the Orlando airport after she finished working," he says. "She is leaving dad and going to Atlanta, Georgia, to start a new life. She will be back to get the both of you in about two weeks, once she gets herself situated." I am totally speechless and I don't say another word, all the way to the house.

I run into the house and go from room to room, frantically looking for my mom, but she's not here. I go into her bedroom and open up the closet to find that all her clothes are still here. I can't believe that she is gone, so I close myself up inside the closet and fall upon the floor. I begin to cry, and cry, and cry, until I cry myself to sleep.

Kirkwood

"Sergio, Sergio, wake up, wake up, Sergio, we're here. We're in Atlanta, Sergio," my brother Rob keeps repeating. Finally, after the longest two weeks of anticipating seeing my mom and enduring the longest ride of my life, I awaken. I sit in the backseat of Claude's car and look out of the window. "Wow, look at the freaking buildings, Rob. We are in the city now," I say to my younger brother. I have never seen this many black people walking and driving around before; everywhere I look, I can see them. It's almost as if I'm in another world, like I've been born again.

Claude is married to my mom's cousin Esther, and he was nice enough to drive all the way to Florida to pick us up. We are going to be staying with them and their three kids, Regina, Clint, and Ricky. They have four other children, Toot, Sister, Bud, and Shirley, but they are all grown and out of the house.

Claude and Esther live in a beautiful big house on Sisson Avenue, in the metropolitan area of Atlanta. The house is only five minutes away from downtown, and I can literally see the top of some of the buildings from the street. Claude also has his own business, cleaning banks after business hours, and he seems to have done very well for himself.

As soon as I finish hugging my mom and telling her how much that I miss her, I can hear my cousin Clint calling me. "Sergio, Sergio, come on, man, come on, and play football with us." I agree to join them, and I'm thinking that we're about to go into one of the neighbors' backyard, but no, they play in the middle of the street.

The cars literally have to wait until the end of the play in order to pass through. There is no tackling; only shoving is allowed on the street to avoid anyone from being seriously injured.

On the very first play, I'm placed on defense, and I line up in front of the wide receiver to defend against the pass. "Down, set, hut one, hut two." *Bam!* I try to take this guy's head off as he comes off the line. "Oh shit!" somebody screams. "The Florida boy wants to play rough." Ironically, the guy I just knocked to the ground has the same name as my dad, Roy.

"Roy, Roy, what's up man? Don't tell me that you are going to let the new kid hit you like that and get away with it," his brother asks. "No, I'm going to kick his ass," Roy says to his brother. I prepare myself to fight, and I'm waiting on him to get within striking distance because when he does, I am going to throw the first punch.

He quickly realizes that I am not going to back down, so he changes his mind about fighting me. "The new kid doesn't take any shit," somebody in the crowd shouts out loud. Looks like Roy has met his match.

I realize now that Roy is the little neighborhood bully, and all the kids are scared of him. I have instantly gained respect from all of them because I am standing up to him and ready to fight. Roy seems to be caught off guard with my courage and decides to back down. As I walk away from the situation, I'm thinking, *Damn, I've only been here for an hour and almost got into a fight already.*

As the weeks go by, everything is going great; we all are getting along well. Clint, Ricky, Rob, and I are all sleeping in the same bedroom, so we get into little arguments here and there but never anything serious enough to fight about it. I like Clint and Rick, so if anything goes down in the street, I'll be right there to have their backs.

My dad was nice enough to bring my mom a car here for us to get around in, once he came to the realization that she is not returning to Florida. As we get into the car on our way to register for school, I start to feel a little nervous. Clint has told me a lot about the school, and from the information that he gave me, it's going to be quite a challenge for me, being that I'm the new kid.

As we pull up to the school, I am amazed at how many kids are here, and they're all black too. I have never seen this many blacks in one place in all my life, so I'm happy and scared at the same time. "Hey, Sergio, just relax and carry yourself the same way you do at home in the street, and everything will be all right," my cousin Clint says.

Girls, girls, girls, they are all over the place. I'm going to have a field day at this school concerning the girls because I am already getting some flirts. The girls here are more conscious and concerned about how they look, compared to the girls in Florida.

They are so pretty, with their hair pressed and styled; even their fingernails and toes are painted. There is a big difference between city girls and country girls, and I like what I see in the city girls.

Clint's older sister Shirley is a hairstylist, and she works at a salon right down the street from the house. I'm going to ask her to give me a blowout hairstyle. It's a new style that all the guys are wearing. My hair will have to be processed with a relaxer, blown dry with a blow-dryer, and cut to perfection. Once I get my hairstyle together, I'll be ready to start flirting with some girls.

My mom has found a job, but I want to pay Shirley with money that I earn myself. Claude has about ten banks that he cleans up at night, and he has been letting me go with him to earn some cash. I must say that I'm impressed because I have never seen a nigga with keys to open up a bank before; they must really trust Claude. I should have enough money to get my hair done in about two weeks, and I'm excited.

Esther has a brother named Johnny, who lives in the house also, and I'm scared to death of him. He has burns all over his face and body from a fire, and the way he looks just scares the shit out of me. He never goes outside, and he sits in the back room all day, drinking liquor to the point where he can't walk. I've seen him urinate on himself numerous times, because he's too drunk to make it to the bathroom. I'm scared of him when he's sober, so when he's drunk, it's terrifying.

When I see him, it makes me think about the devil and the crazy dreams that I still have to endure. It's something about his spirit that bothers me, and he even looks at me as if he knows that I can read his spirit. His face is burned to a crispy black, and all his hair is burned out with the exception of a few strands.

He stays sloppy drunk, so when he tries to speak, his words are slurred, and slobber comes from his mouth, dripping down to his shirt. His eyes are fixed way back into his head, with a red-yellowish color like a demon's. I'm scared of Johnny, so I avoid passing by him throughout the house.

Clint has been telling my brother Rob and I about a gang that goes and takes money from students after school's out. Everybody is afraid of them, including the principal and bus drivers. As the students line up to catch the city buses with fare in hand, the gang goes up and takes their money. If someone doesn't give up the money, then they will get a serious beat-down.

I've been seeing the gang all week, but they have been terrifying different bus routes. Today I got a feeling that they're coming to my bus, and I couldn't be more right because here they come right now. I'm seated at the very back, facing the front of the bus, and the gang is coming straight at me.

"Give me your money," he says to the guy sitting next to me. Before the guy can get his hands out of his pocket, the gang member slapped the spit out of his mouth. The poor guy starts crying, and I feel sorry for him because no one is going to help him.

"What are you looking at, fool?" the gang member asks me. I look him in the eye, but I don't say a word. He launches at me as if he were going to hit me, and I still don't move, so now he's really pissed off. "You think you're tough, huh, little man?" he says to me as he pokes me in the eye with his finger.

I immediately grab my eye from the pain and look at him with the other. The leader of the gang stands up and says, "Fight him or fight me, but you damn sure better not let him get away with that."

Before he can finish that sentence, I'm all over the guy that poked me in the eye. I grab him by the shirt and sling his Little Ass into the steel rail of the bus. He's stunned and motionless, so I put him in a choke hold, using the rail as leverage. I got this dude pinned up, and he can't do anything, not even breathe.

I look around to the front of the bus, and the leader of the gang is running straight toward me with an elbow pad on his arm. He hits me directly on the head with his elbow, and I'm knocked over to the side of the bus. I reach for the stop cable and pull it repeatedly until finally, the driver stops the bus for me to make my escape.

Now here I am, lost, and I don't know the way home; Clint and Rob stayed on the bus. I hope one of them picks up my books because I got off the bus so fast, I didn't have time to pick them up myself. Walking down the boulevard, I see a lot of things going on in the streets. I see the prostitutes on the stroll, drug transactions, gambling, and fighting.

I ask one of the prostitutes to give me directions home, being that I do know the address. Hopefully, I won't run into some neighborhood gang that's angry because I'm passing through their turf.

I finally make it home. Esther and my mom have been riding around, looking for me, worried sick. "I'm all right, I'm all right," I tell them. "A gang of guys from the high school tried to take my money and beat me up, but I was able to get off the bus. Clint and Rob acted like they didn't know me. While I was fighting, I looked over at both of them, and they turned their heads to deny knowing me, just like Peter denied Jesus.

"If the situation was reversed, I would have no problem jumping in a fight to help either one of them. They acted like little punks!"

"Hold it, hold it," my mom says. "I know that you are angry in regards to what happened, but we don't need any name-calling."

"Yes, ma'am, I'm sorry, but I had one of them beat, Mom, until the big guy jumped in to help him. It was only two of them on the bus, so the three of us could have kicked their behinds."

As the weeks go by, I'm starting to feel uncomfortable in certain parts of the house. Maybe it's because of some of the things that I'm starting to discover that's in the house abroad. Some of the items, in my point of view, are affiliated with voodoo.

I don't know much about curses and spells; all I know is that whoever uses it is the devil's advocate. Surreptitiously, someone is trying to keep these items hidden from the rest of the family.

I can remember when we were in Florida that my mom had problems with her leg. She went to the doctor, and he couldn't figure out what was wrong with her. After about three days, my brother Rob couldn't walk. My parents took him to the doctor as well. The doctor could not find the cause of his problem either. I literally had to pick him up and hold him over the toilet in order for him to use the bathroom.

My dad decided to take Mom to a root doctor to seek help. She was told that the hex was too strong for a female to release her from it and that she must find a male to eliminate the hex. Of course, my dad was too jealous to take her to see a man, even though the man was supposedly able to help her.

My mom had to sneak in order to see this so-called root doctor. I don't know what he did, but a couple of days later, she and Rob were back to normal.

So now when I hear people say certain things referring to voodoo, I get uncomfortable because I don't think that they actually realize the power of the subject matter. I feel that Satan has a limited amount of power here on earth. When I pray to God, I expect certain things to happen; that is the power of prayer. So in the same sense, I feel that if someone prays to Satan, certain things can happen as well.

Both Clint and Rick are some spoiled little brats; they're fortunate enough to get everything that they ask for. Esther and Claude rarely deny them of gifts and toys. It seems like every week they have something new. Rob and I have to listen to them brag about this and that all the time. So when one of them screws up and gets in trouble, we sit back and watch the ass whipping they get from Esther.

Esther has never tried to whip Rob or me. Maybe my mom does not agree with someone else punishing us. I'm glad that my mom won't allow it, because when Esther whips Clint, I feel sorry for him. She is almost as bad as my dad concerning whipping her kids.

"Sergio, Rob, come here," my mom calls out. "Get in the car because I have a surprise that I want to show the both of you."

"What is it, Mom? What is it? I love surprises," I reply. "Just get in the car and you will see in a few minutes," she says. After driving for fifteen minutes, we arrive at an apartment, and she tells us to get out. She gives me the key and says, "Open the door because this is our new home and the both of you have your own room."

"Yeah, now that's what I'm talking about, Mom. We got our own place now. Thank you, Jesus. Thank you, Lord." I am so excited that I can barely get the key in the door, and Rob is right behind me, saying, "Open it, open it, Sergio, open it."

As soon as I get inside, I run to the bedroom that I want to claim as mine. I enter into the back bedroom and close the door behind me, then I fall down on my knees and raise my hands to the god I serve and say, "Thank you, Jesus."

Scottdale

Today I am starting at a new school, and it is an integrated school called Clarkston High. When I was in the city of Atlanta, I was going to a middle school, but this year I'm going to high school. Now I have to make friends all over again, when I had just gotten myself familiar with all the niggas in Kirkwood.

I registered myself into their music program, and I want to learn how to play symphony. I've been taking music classes since the fourth grade.

My music skills are very impressive, according to my instructor. He has selected me to play first chair on the trombone. I also play drums and percussion at times. Every time that I take my instrument home on the school bus, all the kids laugh at me because I'm the only black student that studies music in this school. They make a mockery out of me and call me names.

I take it all in without saying a word because they don't realize that one day, I'm going to be somebody. I just know it because God shows me that in my dreams all the time. In my dreams I'm able to fly over people from a running start, and I've seen myself standing in front of thousands of people. I have that dream repetitiously, over and over again. I just wish that I could interpret it.

God shows me visions of things to come, and most of what I see come to pass. Sometimes I wonder if that's the reason why Satan attacks me so often. Is he mad because of my gift from God? Nobody has a clue as to what's going on between God, Satan, and I. It's like a freaking war going on for my very soul; there's something that God has planned for me, and Satan doesn't want to see it happen.

Whatever it is, it has to be something big enough to affect other people; otherwise, what is the point? Why do I feel like a rope being pulled from both ends, God on one and Satan on the other? Why is it that I can see the death of people whom I don't know, and if I focus enough, I can communicate with dead people that I do know?

All these things are strange by nature, so I dare not tell anyone about what's going on. I guess this is a secret that I will take to my grave. My friends always ask me why I don't laugh and smile more often; they say that I look like I'm always thinking about something. They are absolutely right. I am always thinking about something. Most of the time, my thoughts are pleasant, but then again there is a dark side.

The apartment that we live in is very close to the recreation center, and all the kids have to pass by our place en route there. I've been checking out this girl by the name of Stephanie P., and I think she likes me. She always smiles at me when she passes by, and here she comes now. Today is the day that I'm going to make my move on her.

"Hey, Stephanie, what's happening, girl? How are you doing?" is what I say to her. "Hi, Sergio," she replies with a huge blush on her face. It's so noticeable because of her light skin.

Stephanie has beautiful, sexy big lips, and she knows it. I have never seen her without lip gloss. As I slowly look at her up and down, I ask, "Can I come by your way a little later to sit with you and talk?" She looks me in the eye and says, "Sure, seven thirty because at nine o'clock I will be going to bed." Immediately she starts walking away from me, I watch her shake her tight little ass for about fifty feet, and then say, "Cool, I'll be there."

When I arrive at Stephanie's place, she is dressed in shorts with a white T-shirt. I can see her hard red nipples standing in attention as they press against the shirt so tightly. Her legs are long, sleek, and greased down from her ass to her toes; she's looking hot.

She immediately introduces me to her six sisters, and all of them are fine and cute. Her mother is a single parent, so I'm surrounded by females, and I have no problem with that.

Finally, after meeting her family, we get a little privacy. We look into each other's eyes before slowly moving toward each other; then the kissing starts. The kissing progresses into touching, the touching progresses into grinding, and now I'm snatching her little shorts down because I know she's ready.

She makes no attempt to stop me from advancing further, so eventually we make passionate love on the floor of the living room. It's quick, like *wham*, *bam*, thank you, ma'am. Damn, I am not trying to get caught with my pants down.

Months go by and Stephanie and I are still kicking it strong. I see her at least five nights per week. She gets mad at me about smoking weed with my boys. It's five of us, and we get high every day. Kenny Davis, Gerald Jones, Johnny Ray, Dennis Moss, and I are a unit. We smoke weed before school, and we smoke weed after school.

When we get on the bus in the mornings for school, everyone can smell the aroma of the red bud. We're always in good spirits, laughing and talking shit, flirting with the girls, and pissing off the guys. We chip in two dollars each and get a dime bag every morning. From that dime bag we roll up ten joints and smoke all day till night. Mom has been checking me lately by asking why my eyes are red.

I just tell her that I'm tired, and go to my room. She works late, so by the time she gets home, I have the place cleaned spick-and-span, with dinner on the stove. I learned how to cook from watching her, and I've become quite good at it.

It makes her happy to come home and not have to do any work. I always have it all taken care of. "Sergio, Sergio, you are going to make some lucky lady happy one day" is what she always tells me.

The unit and I just finished smoking a couple of joints, and we're headed to Mrs. Dorothy's store to buy pig-ear sandwiches, smothered with chili, onions, and mustard. With a cold cream soda out of her ice chest, you just can't beat it for a Munchies, buster. On our way back from Mrs. Dorothy's store, I see this pretty little redbone, so I walk up to her and boldly introduce myself.

She says her name is Irish A. and that I can call her later. While gazing into her beautiful hazel eyes, I softly reply, "I'll be sure to do that."

As I start to walk away, I wonder how I would feel if Stephanie saw someone else. I probably wouldn't like it at all. Nevertheless, I am going to call Irish A. Once we get back to Tobie Grant, we go into the recreation center to partake in a game of basketball.

I'm running down the court to get back on defense. The shot goes up; it's a miss, and I reach up to snatch the rebound. As I turn around with the ball to dribble up court, out of nowhere comes Iron Head. He's not a part of the game. This fool is just trying to get away from somebody, and he can't see me. *Bang!* His head hits me straight in the mouth. The impact is so hard that everyone inside the gym freezes.

I'm knocked to the floor, and blood is just pouring out of my mouth. I look around and see my tooth on the floor; it's been knocked out of my mouth from the root, and it's almost four inches long. I can't feel anything with my tongue as I move it around the top of my mouth, so now I'm scared to death. I get up and run, and run, as fast as I can, nonstop, until I make it to the front door of our apartment.

"Sergio, Sergio, Lord have mercy, child, what has happened to you? Jesus," Mom says. She grabs a towel to cover my mouth and rushes me to the hospital. The doctor takes one look at me and says, "Set him up for surgery." The nurse says, "All right, Sergio, I'm going to give you a little shot here to make you relax." Shortly after the shot, I start feeling sleepy, and sleepy, until I am fast asleep.

When I finally wake up, my mom is sitting next to me, and she says, "It's going to be all right, sweetie. Just try to get some rest." Slowly and reluctantly, I move my tongue around my mouth, and all I can feel are wire and stitches.

I rise up from the bed frantically with tears in my eyes to ask her, "What have they done to me?" To my surprise, no words are coming out, I'm just mumbling. Now I'm really freaked out because I can't understand my own words.

The collision between Iron Head and me keeps repeating itself in my head even though weeks have passed. I'm very frustrated because the only way that I can consume food is by using a straw, so my diet is very limited and I am not happy about it.

The doctor said that it would be months before I can bite down on anything. The wires are literally holding my teeth in place. Not only that, but I have stitches in my lip, and it's very irritating. I have never been this embarrassed and humiliated before. I feel like I just want to hide from the world.

After months of me suffering pain and being embarrassed to smile, the time finally comes for me to pick up my partial plate with an artificial tooth attached. It took me a long time to convince my mom to let me get a gold tooth. I had been asking her about it for months.

The dentist carefully installs the plate and proudly passes me a mirror. As I slowly start to smile, I can see the gold twinkling like bling-bling from the bright lights in the room.

Damn, that looks pretty cool, and I'm going to be the only guy in high school with a gold tooth. I'm back in full effect, so look out, girls. Here I come. First thing on my agenda is to call the unit so I can smoke some weed and catch a buzz; afterward I'm going to see Stephanie. I haven't seen her for months because I have been too embarrassed for anyone to see me.

Weeks pass by and I finally decide to give Irish a call to invite her to the crib. I picked a perfect day because Mom is not at home, nor is Stephanie in the neighborhood. Irish comes to my door, looking all cute and fine with her nails freshly done and lip gloss on her lips, so I waste no time getting her inside. She says, "Sergio, I am a virgin and I've never been with a guy before, so please be gentle with me."

Now I have two girlfriends, one in Tobie Grant and another on Cedar Street. I see each one of them three times per week, so they have been keeping me pretty busy. There is a church directly across the street from our apartment, and every Sunday the street is packed with cars. I know that I should be going to church to listen to the Word, but instead I sit on the porch and flirt with the girls passing by.

As I sit here on the porch, looking at all the finely dressed people going inside the church, I ask myself, Is it absolutely necessary for me to go to church in order to have a relationship with God? I feel as if I'm disappointing him at times.

I know that the Holy Spirit dwells inside me because I can feel his presence. When I get in the spirit, my body tingles from my head to my toe, and my heart explodes with love. I speak in different tongues, and I know that God is listening to me.

I am very capable now of reading and feeding off someone else's spirit. I'm finally figuring out how to use this gift that my grandmother says I have. All I have to do is focus in the spirit, and things are revealed back to me, in the spirit. It's like the invisible world that most people aren't aware of.

I guess the best way to describe this gift is to say that I'm very intuitive and then some. God shows me visions of some things to come and protects me from evil. He has also given me the ability to discern spirits of people that I come in contact with. I am trying to learn how to interpret the things that I see in my dreams; only then, maybe, can I help someone in some type of way spiritually.

Time moves on and I have become pretty popular in Scottdale. I know a lot of people. I know all the drug dealers in this area, and I can get you anything that you desire through my contacts.

I only smoke weed, but I have access to cocaine, heroin, pills, and anything else you may want to get high from. All the dealers think that I'm cool and trustworthy, and a couple of them ask me to sell their drugs, but I declined.

I don't want people coming to my mom's apartment, knocking on her door, looking for drugs. She would be so angry and disappointed in me if that were to ever happen. Today the unit and I skipped school. We have been having fun all day smoking weed and going to different places on the bus.

We finally get back in the neighborhood before school is let out, and I decide to take them to our apartment. I go into my bedroom and come back out with a fresh smoking pipe that I made in art class. Everybody wants to smoke out of the pipe, so Dennis reaches into his pocket and pulls out the weed. As we sit there enjoying our buzz, suddenly I hear a car pull up in front of the apartment.

Oh shit, it's my mom, and she has come home three hours early today. The unit is scrambling to get out of the back door while I'm trying to get rid of the evidence. Just as the last guy runs out of the back door, I can hear her keys turning the lock at the front door.

"Sergio, what are you doing here and why are you not in school?" she asks. Before I can answer the question, she says, "I smell something burning, and I saw those kids run out of my back door. Have you guys been smoking dope in here? Oh, Lord, have mercy, Jesus," she says. "Boy, you done got yourself on them drugs."

21

She immediately starts crying, and then she starts shouting at me. "Sergio, you are going to have to get the hell out of here," she says, "because I am not going to put up with you smoking dope in my house. I'm going to call your daddy right now and have him to come and get you. Maybe he can straighten you out," she says.

"Oh no, Mom, I don't want to go back to Tavares. Please don't make me do that. I won't smoke any more weed. Just give me another chance, I'm sorry."

"No, Sergio, you are going back to Florida with your daddy, and you are not going to make me change my mind either. Go back there in your room somewhere because I don't even want to see your face right now. I can't believe you," she says.

I go in my room and close the door behind me. Oh shit, I'm going back to the freaking country. Are you serious.? Oh, hell no, she's got to be kidding me. I do not want to go back to Florida around all those old crackers.

As I come out of the room and start down the hallway to the front door, I can hear my mom on the phone, talking to my dad. I guess this means she is serious, and I'm going back to Florida for sure. Now I'm thinking about when I arrived here and how I felt as if I were born again. Now that I'm leaving, I feel as if I'm dead again.

Florida

Within a matter of days, I found myself on Interstate 75 south, crossing the Florida line with my dad. He has already laid down all the rules of his house while driving back. I don't like this at all, but I'm going to have to make the best out of it.

The rules are not that bad, and I'm going to be the only child in the house with him. My sister, Betty, is married, Ronald is in the army, and Donnie has graduated and enlisted in the army also.

I am sixteen years old now, so the first thing that I have on my agenda here is getting my dad to find me a car. Both of my brothers were driving their own cars at the age of sixteen, so now it's my turn.

I already know that he is going to make me work for it, and that's just fine with me. I wouldn't want it any other way. I would much rather work and pay for it myself than to have someone else do it who would then get angry with me later and try to take it from me.

I know one damn thing for sure: I am too big for that whipping shit now, so I wonder how he's going to come at me now when he gets mad. It better not be with a weapon of any sort because I will defend myself to the fullest. I just spent four years away from him in Atlanta, and I am definitely not the little kid that he remembers.

I'm sure that he has no idea as to what kind of things I've seen or people I've known in Atlanta. I feel like I have been put back in time here because these old crackers have not changed a bit. They are still racist, and these niggas still put up with their shit. This is not going to work out for me because there is going to be a big problem as soon as one of them disrespects me.

At school the white girls seem to be just as interested in me as the sisters. I get a lot of flirts and attention from both of them, and the principal does not like it. I can tell that he has a problem with me, just by the look in his eyes.

My football coach gives me the same look; he can't stand me, but he has to acknowledge my physical ability.

I am a starter on defense at the cornerback position, and anybody that comes my way is subject to getting their head knocked off. I release a lot of anger when I am on the field, and no one is an exception to the rule. I'm also playing on special teams. I am in the deep position on kickoff and punt returns.

It's Friday night, and tonight is our first game of the season against Mount Dora. We win the toss, and Mount Dora has to kick us the ball. It's a high, long kick, but it's going straight to Irvin Smith, my teammate on the other side of the field. The lights are bright and the crowd is screaming as the ball is caught by Irvin.

I am Irvin's last line of defense, so I take off in front of him to be his lead blocker. We're at the twenty, twenty-five, thirty, thirty, thirty-five forty, *boom!* I hit this white boy so hard that the sound of the impact is heard by everyone in the stadium.

The crowd stands up, and I can hear some of the people saying, "Oh shit, what a hit." As I start to get off the guy that I just buried, he grabs me by the face mask and pulls me back down. He punches me in the stomach several times, and the referee, standing right next to us, doesn't even throw a flag.

I look over at the referee and ask, "Are you going to throw the flag or what?" And he doesn't respond to me. I turn and look at the white boy that just punched me, and he is still lying on his back. I grab him by his face mask, snatch him up, and knock him back down to the field with one punch.

"Lovett, Lovett, Lovett, get out of there! What do you think you are doing, son?" the coach shouts at me. "The guy punched me in the stomach twice right in front of the referee," I replied. The coach looks at me and says, "Get out of my gear and go sit in the stands, I don't want you on this team." I look at him straight in the eye and say, "No problem, I'll take your shit off."

The coach pissed me off so bad with his response to the situation that I didn't feel comfortable sitting in the stands, supporting the team. Instead I started focusing on one of the other team cheerleaders. Wow, she is very pretty. She is so tall and slim, dark skinned, with silky long hair, beautiful big eyes, and a smile to die for. I must get her phone number before she gets back on the bus to leave.

She is checking me out just as much as I'm checking her, and we have made eye contact with each other several times. The game is over now, and she is coming to the bus where I'm posted up already. As she approaches, I smile at her and say, "Hello, I know that this is a little strange being that you are with the other team, but I was wondering if you would give me your number so that I can call you."

She smiles even more and says, "Sure, my name is Sarah, and yes, I'll give you my number." So I ask her, "Sarah, when is the best time to call you?" She said, "You can call me tonight, Sergio. I'll be home in about one hour." After one hour passes, I call her, and we engage in a long conversation about the game and other issues. I think Sarah really likes me, and I am excited about her.

A couple of weeks pass by, and before you know it, my dad and I are standing in front of a blue 1968 Chevrolet Camaro. I have been telling him about this car for months, and today I have the money in my hand to buy it. I'm about two hundred dollars short of the asking price, and I'm hoping that he will give me or let me borrow the rest.

The car has a fresh new paint job on it, and it is clean inside and out. It has two white stripes down the center of the hood to match the white interior of the car. My dad looks at the car then looks at me and says, "If you don't do right, I am going to take it from you." He gives me the two hundred dollars, and I make the transaction.

As I'm driving away from Wheeler's Paint Shop, where I just bought the car, I'm thinking to myself, *Sarah, here I come. Tonight it's going to be on.* I get home and clean the car up even more, then I call up Sarah. She says, "Cool, Sergio, I will see you when you get here."

I take a shower and get myself all cleaned up and head out the door. Before I go to Mount Dora, I stop in Tavares at the basketball court and smoke a couple of joints with George Dixon. He's my smoke buddy now.

George asks, "Hey, man, is that your ride.?" I reply, "You know us Lovett boys. We have got to be riding when we turn sixteen."

"Damn, man, that's a pretty car. It looks like it has just been painted."

"Yeah, it's all right, and it runs good too," I reply. So we crank up the music and fire up the weed. George knows that my favorite bands are the Isley Brothers and the Bar-Kays, so he gives me a Bar-Kays tape to keep in my ride.

Sarah and I have been talking on the phone with each other for weeks, and now I'm standing at her front door. She greets me with a hug followed by the introduction to her mom, Bennie, and her sister, Gloria. Sarah is a very pretty and smart girl, and I can sense that she is a virgin. I know that this girl is not going to be easy for me to conquer, so my conduct is nothing less than that of a perfect little gentleman.

She walks with me to check out my ride in the parking lot, and she's impressed. "Let's go for a little ride," she says. "We can go and grab something to eat and then come back to watch a movie." Sarah takes driver education classes at my school, and her teacher just so happens to be my ex–football coach. She says, "The coach told me that I'm too nice of a girl to go out with you and that you have a bad attitude."

I respond by saying, "Yes, I do have a bad attitude if someone grabs me by my face mask and punches me in the stomach." She starts laughing and says, "I guess you have a point because I saw the whole thing, and they should've thrown a flag when the guy punched you first. They are still talking about the block that you put on that guy. Everybody in the stadium heard the sound of that hit."

After eating our meal and watching a movie, finally I get the chance to put the moves on Sarah. She is very receptive to my kisses and hugs, but she will not allow me to touch her anywhere below the belt. I like that about her, and I know that she is going to be a serious challenge for me. Most girls submit to me once I have them alone, but not Sarah; she is not going to be easy by any means.

In Tavares High School, I am the only black student that has a car. The other black students are envious of me, and the white boys are jealous. The only sense of approval I get while I'm in school comes from white females. They are all over me and constantly flirting with me. The principal has noticed the attention that I'm getting, and he doesn't like it at all.

"Lovett, I need to see you in my office," he says. "Well, what is this all about, sir?" I ask him. "Just be in my office by the time I get there," he says. So here I am sitting in his office, without a clue as to why he wants me here. He steps in the lobby and signals by using his head and finger for me to go into his office.

"Lovett, I have been noticing that you leave the school campus for lunch in your vehicle," he says. "That privilege is only for the seniors at this school, and you are in violation of school policy. This is a warning, and the next time I see you leave campus for lunch, I will suspend you."

"Well, sir, I am not the only junior that has a car and leave the campus for lunch," I reply. "Granted that I am the only black student with a car, would you, by chance, be singling me out, sir?" I ask. "Lovett, get out of my office," he says.

"I can't believe this cracker," I say to myself as I exit his office. My grandmother's house is three blocks away, and my aunt Sadie's house is just as close. I usually go to one of their homes and grab a quick sandwich, and afterward I stop by the juke joint and smoke. This is going to mess up my midday buzz; now I have to deal with these crackers all day on a straightened arrow.

Finally it's the weekend, and my brother Donnie is here from the army. Oh shit, his ride is so fly. It is a 1973 Oldsmobile Cutlass. It has a fresh burgundy paint job, new white leather top, new white leather interior, and freaking gangster whitewall tires. He throws me the keys and says, "I'm going to be leaving my car with you for a while, so take good care of it."

"Are you serious? You're going to leave that car with me?" I ask. "Yes," he says, "I have to go away for thirty days, and I would feel more comfortable with you having it than for it to be sitting in a parking lot."

"Cool," I reply, "I'll take good care of it. You see that Camaro out there, don't you?"

Two days later, Donnie is gone, and I'm switching cars every time I change clothes. These crackers and niggas don't know what to think of me. I'm just shining all the time, and a lot of people don't like it. That's why I spend most of my time in Mount Dora with Sarah. She finally submitted herself to me, and it's been love since.

Today I don't feel like going to school, so I'm going to skip all my classes and chill out uptown. I run into George at the usual spot, the basketball court. He throws newspapers early in the morning, and when he finishes, he always parks his van at the court to sit and smoke weed. I jump into the van with him, and he immediately ejects a tape out of the deck. He looks at me and says, "Pass me your shit, the Bar-Kays."

"Holy Ghost" happens to be my most favorite track on the tape. George has it turned up as loud as his stereo will play, as we puff away on a fat joint. "Oh shit," George says, "here comes your pop, and he don't look happy." George is right; my dad is pulling up in the service truck on me like he's the freaking police.

I'm embarrassed, and I don't want this confrontation to happen in the streets. So I jump out of George's van and quickly get into my car and leave. I drive straight to the house and wait for him boldly because he is not going to whip me again, ever. He comes in the house and says, "This is not going to work out. I don't have time to be leaving my job to chase you around town when you should be at school."

Weeks pass, and I have been doing pretty good about not leaving campus. Today is going to have to be an exception because I am hungry and I have no lunch money. So I sneak to my car at lunchtime and go to my grandmother's house for a sandwich. I run into Doyle Lane on my way back, and he smokes a joint with me followed by a shot of liquor.

Once I get back on campus, I try to sneak my car back into the parking lot without being noticed. I make it back to class on time, but the teacher stops me and says, "Lovett, have you been drinking? I smell alcohol."

"No, I haven't," I reply, and I proceed to take my seat. "Lovett, excuse me," she says, "I think you need to go to the principal's office."

I have been sitting here in the lobby of the principal's office for thirty minutes, then suddenly he opens his door and says, "Lovett, get in here." He looks at me and asks, "Lovett, have you been drinking, and did you leave the campus for lunch?"

"Yes, I did leave the campus for lunch because I didn't have money to eat here. No, I have not been drinking," I reply. Without a second thought, this cracker says, "You are expelled from this school, and I need you to get off of the property."

Oh shit, I'm in big trouble this time. Dad is going to be pissed. To my surprise, he doesn't shout at me; he just says, "Boy, I guess you're going to have to go back to Atlanta to finish school." I play it off as if I'm disappointed, but what he just said is music to my ears. Hot damn, I'm going back to Atlanta, and this time I have a car. Oh shit, now I feel like I'm born again.

After talking with Dad, I jump in the car and go straight to Wheeler Auto Body Shop. Mr. Wheeler's son, Mark, wants my Camaro. He has a 1967 Ford Mustang GT, and it just came out of the paint booth with a fresh candy-apple-red paint job. The Mustang has a V-8 engine, which is a lot more powerful than my Camaro's straight six-cylinder engine. Mark wants my Camaro for the body, and today we're making an even swap.

The Dale

Damn, I hate to leave Sarah because she is definitely in love with me, and I think I love her too. She cried like a baby when I told her the news, and that hit me right in the heart. I had tears in my eyes as well as I said good-bye to her. I will always have love for Sarah because we shared some very special times together.

I have the car packed, gassed up, cleaned up, and ready to roll. My dad comes out of the house and breaks bread with me and wishes me luck as I pull out of the driveway. I cruise slowly through Leesburg and Wildwood, but when I get to Interstate 75 north, I'm pushing ninety miles per hour. I pinch myself because damn, I'm only sixteen years old driving a pretty-ass Mustang by myself on the way back to the Dale.

It was a long ride, but finally I'm back in the Dale, pulling up in front of Mom's apartment. As I unload my stuff out of the car, Rob is admiring the paint job. "Damn, Sergio," he says, "this car is pretty, man. You're going to be on them now, sonny."

I greet Mom, and she appears to be glad to see me, so that's a good sign. I can't believe that she's not drilling me on the fact that I got kicked out of school in Florida. She just smiles and hugs me then asks, "Are you hungry, Sergio?"

"No, ma'am, I ate on the way here," I reply. As soon as I finished unpacking my gear, I hit the shower and get fresh.

First stop, Rob and I hit the car wash to get all the highway dust off the Mustang. We end up in Kirkwood to visit my aunt Esther and family. Clint and Rick are happy to see me, and we all go into the backyard and blow a couple of joints. Clint brings me up to speed on everything that's been going on in Kirkwood. Things have changed a lot because we're all a little older, and we're trying to do grown-folks shit now.

I drop Rob off at the crib, and to Stephanie's place I go. *Knock, knock, knock.* "Who is it?" she says. "Open this door, girl," I reply. "Sergio, Sergio, hey, baby, when did you get here?" she asks as she jumps up and throws her arms around my neck and her legs around my waist.

Before I can answer her, she has already planted those glossy big lips over mine. "Oh shit, girl, I miss you too." She looks at me and asks, "Is that your ride sitting out there?"

"Yes, it is," I say to her. "So come on and roll with me for a minute."

"Sure, just give me a moment to freshen up," she says. "Where are we going, by the way?"

"Downtown on Peachtree Street, from Five Points to Buckhead," I tell her. "I need to see the city lights again because it's been a long time for me." As I approach downtown, I realize how blessed I am to be back in the city. The opportunity here is unlimited; my success or failure depends on me.

The next day before I can get out of bed and get dressed, the unit is knocking at the door. "What's happening, bro?" they all say with a hand slap. "Hey, I'm back, nigga, live and in color, so what's shaking?" I ask them. "There's going to be a house party tonight on the other side of the hill, and you know all the girls in the Dale is going to be there."

"Man, I just seen Stephanie last night," I tell them. "So you know that she's going to be all up on me." Dennis says, "Yeah, and you have that pretty ride too. Stephanie is not about to let you ride another girl in that car, and you better believe that."

"I'm cool, man. I'm cool," I tell them. "I'm not trying to hit every girl in the freaking neighborhood."

So the unit and I walk to the park and catch up on old times while smoking a couple of joints. The police rarely come through our neighborhood, so we can smoke just about anywhere that we want to. Afterward, I head back home to get my car cleaned up for the party tonight.

As soon as I get to the party and step out of the car, I can sense that something is wrong. The party is in the house, the party is in the street, these niggas are everywhere. I can see about three different gangs here, so I know that it's going to be some trouble.

Stephanie just noticed me, so I signal for her to come to the car. "Hey, baby, get in the car because it's about to be some shit go down very shortly," I say to her. "All right, Sergio, I don't want to be around when that happens, so let's go," she says.

Before we can get out of the parking space, the fighting erupts from inside the house. From the house, they move to the street, and it must be twenty or more guys involved. Stephanie looks at me and says, "Damn, Sergio, you said that there was going to be some trouble."

We end up at her place for a quiet evening inside, just talking to each other.

The fighting can go on for hours and cross many blocks, so it is best for us to stay inside the house tonight.

Months later, it is Christmas time in the city, my most favorite holiday. I love the joy of giving and seeing happiness on the face of others. Jesus is the reason for the season, and I love celebrating his birthday.

My mom bought me an electric bass guitar with an amplifier, and I am on cloud nine right now. This is the instrument that I keep seeing myself play in my dreams; now I finally have it in my hands. I'm going to teach myself how to play this bass, no matter how long it takes me.

Christmas was fantastic, and today is January 1, 1977. "Happy New Year" is all that I've been hearing for the past twenty-four hours. There were parties everywhere last night, and I had a very good time.

I'm waking up late from a slight hangover. I normally don't drink alcohol, but last night was an exception. *Ring, ring, ring.* Oh shit, the freaking phone sounds as loud as a church bell. I have a headache, and I must take something for it.

"Mom, Mom, will you please answer that phone so that it will stop ringing? If someone is calling for me, just tell them that I will call them back later."

"Hello, hello," she says as she answers the phone. All of a sudden, she starts screaming and crying, "Lord Jesus, Lord Jesus, oh no, Lord Jesus."

"What's wrong, Mom? Mom, what's wrong? What is it?" I ask. She's on her knees, and I have never seen her cry like this before, so now I'm really getting scared. "What's wrong, Mom? What's wrong?" I ask again.

Sobbing and barely able to speak, she slowly grabs me by my hand and looks me in the eyes and says, "Sergio, I'm so sorry, honey, but your grandmother just passed away." I'm in shock and I can't even speak, so I just stand there motionless, with tears running down my face.

My mom grabs a hold of me and hugs me while we cry together. I feel as if I'm about to explode from the love that I have for my grandmother. I don't want to believe that she's gone.

The next day we are in Florida; everybody is at my grandmother's house. There are so many people here because my grandmother is well liked by everyone that knows her. After church the preacher never goes straight home; he and the deacons always go by Granny Rosa's house to eat. I have never heard my grandmother use profanity or a foul word; she's always too busy singing "Amazing Grace" all day.

I just found out that my grandmother died from a heart attack, caused by trying to stop my two grown-ass cousins from fighting. My aunt Sadie has two sons, John, who is in the army, and Charles, who is in the navy.

They were at Granny Rosa's house and got into it about something stupid, arguing with each other and on the verge of fighting each other. All the commotion was more than my grandmother could handle.

I can't believe that they are that stupid and disrespectful. They should have never been fighting in Granny Rosa's house. This house is holy. Now I'm pissed off at both of them, knowing that they're responsible for Granny Rosa's death.

Neither one of them better not say shit to me right now because if they do, I'm going to really go off the deep end. I can't even look at them two niggas right now; they freaking make me sick.

Today is the day of the funeral, and by far it has to be the saddest day of my life. Everybody is crying as they grieve, and I'm absorbing all their pain as well as my own. As I stand over her casket to look at her for the last time, I feel her spirit as she touches me. Her spirit runs through my body as a brisk wind on a cool autumn day. At that very moment I knew that she would be with me always.

It's a long, quiet, and exhausting ride on the way back to Georgia. After seven hours of driving, finally we make it back home in the Dale. It's late, so I go straight to the shower, and then jump in my bed to get some sleep.

As I lie there, I can feel someone else is in the room, watching over me, and not being afraid this time, I slowly open my eyes. It's Granny Rosa, and she's just sitting in the corner of my room in a rocking chair.

"Hey, Granny," I say to her excitedly in a whispered voice. She doesn't respond to me verbally, but she's communicating with my spirit as she begins to hum "Amazing Grace." She's telling me that the Lord has a calling on my life. She says that she will be watching over me and praying over me, always.

As I begin to say thank you, her spirit starts to slowly fade away. Now I feel the Holy Ghost inside me rising up, and it's trying to come out.

Months pass by and I'm still devastated about my grandmother's death. She comes to visit me periodically, mostly when I'm down in spirit. I have distanced myself from the unit and hanging out in the streets. I now spend most of my time playing the bass guitar and trying to compose my own music. I play my bass guitar so long that my mother has to literally come and take it out of my hands once I fall asleep with it in my arms.

I have three bass players that inspire me to practice every time I listen to their music. Stanley Clark, William Collins, and Larry Graham are my favorites, so when I hear those guys play bass guitar, I realize how much I need to practice.

"Wake up, Sergio, wake up, and get ready for school," my mom shouts as she leaves out the door for work. I open my eyes, and to no surprise, lying next to me is my bass guitar. I was up most of the night practicing, so no, I am not going to school today. I get up out of bed anyway, knowing damn well that I have no intentions on going to school.

When I get outside and get into my car, I see two guys coming up the street. Oh shit, it's Gerald Jones and Stan Hicks. Apparently they have skipped school also. We decide to go to a different high school just to flirt with some of their girls before class starts.

Once the first-period bell started ringing for class, everybody began vacating the hallways. Gerald, Stan, and I are on our way out of the school when all of a sudden, Gerald says, "Damn, somebody left their shit in the hallway." It is two trumpets and a saxophone, in hard shell cases. Gerald grabs the trumpets, and Stan grabs the saxophone, then the both of them start running to my car, saying, "Come on, come on, fool, run!"

I run to the car as well with nothing in my hand except the car keys. We manage to get out of there without anyone noticing us, I think. We take the instruments straight to the dope man to trade off for money and weed. When he sees the instruments, his eyes light up like a hundred-watt bulb about to blow. "Damn," he says, "I don't want to know where they came from. All I want to know is how much do you want for this shit."

Before we can answer him, he says, "All right, I'll give each of you twenty dollars in cash and a dime bag of weed for now. The next seven days, each of you can come and get a dime bag of weed every day on me."

"Cool," we tell him, and we all walk out the door, happy and talking shit. We pitch in and pay someone to buy us a twelve-pack of beer and proceed to get wasted.

I make it back to the crib before my mom gets home from work. Thirty minutes after she arrives, there is a knock on the door. "Who is it?" she says in a very subtle voice. "It's the DeKalb County Police, can we please speak with you a moment?" Once inside, they ask me about the instruments. They say that the security guard wrote down my tag number.

I deny having anything to do with the stolen instruments and tell them that there must be a mistake. The detective says, "Young man, if you cooperate and return the instruments, the school will not press charges against you."

"Yeah right," I say to myself. This cracker must think that I'm stupid enough to fall for that shit. If I admit to taking part of that crime, they are going to lock my ass up, period.

I am not giving up anything, so after fifteen minutes of questioning me, he finally decides to leave. I watch him as he leaves our place and then go next door to speak with Gerald. After an hour passes, Gerald and I meet up to discuss our plan; we have to stick together on this one. We talk it over and decide to stick with the story of denial; we didn't do it.

A month has passed, and these cops are still trying to convince our mothers to get us to return the instruments. I keep telling her, "I don't have them, Mom, and I didn't take them." Technically I'm telling her the truth because I did not pick the instruments up, nor do I have them in my possession.

After denying the facts for a couple of months, the detective decides to take me to court. He gives me a court date that's two months away and tells my mom that if I'm convicted, I could be facing some serious time. Now she's aggravating the hell out of me about joining the army. My cousin Shirley is married to an army recruiter, and he told my mom that if I enlist before court date, I won't have to appear in court.

Finally, after listening to my mom nagging me for weeks about the army, I decide to enlist. I drive to downtown Decatur and meet Shirley's husband, Sergeant Pitt, in his office. He tries to make the experience as comfortable as possible because he knows that I'm actually being forced to join. Finishing the paperwork and walking out of the door of his office is strange; now I feel like I don't own myself. I am now property of the United States Army.

Army

"Get out of the bus, get out of the bus, move it, move it, move it, you mama's boy. Didn't you hear me? I said move it, move it, move it!" Damn, am I freaking dreaming, or is this shit for real? I got this big cracker in my face with a hat on like Smokey the Bear, screaming at me. They are rounding us up like cattle going out to slaughter. None of us know what's going to happen next.

They cut my hair, gave me all kinds of shots, issued me uniforms, and completed all the incoming processing before the end of the day. This is serious business; I can't just change my mind and then say that I want to go home. It's November of 1977, and I am in Fort Knox, Kentucky, freezing my ass off. It is thirty-seven degrees here on a good day, and I'm wishing that I were at home, warm, smoking a joint.

I find the weapons training and classes to be very interesting, but being outside for hours marching and running in the snow is no joke. On some days, it takes everything that I have within me to make it through. The physical training is very tough.

These fools wake us up at five o'clock in the morning and expect us to run five miles, in thirty-degree weather. Then later that day, we march in the snow for hours to learn about formations.

The cold weather has literally made me sick. I am in the hospital now with the flu, and it is a very severe case of it. I have been here for two weeks and I am not getting any better; actually I'm getting worse. I am so weak that I can't pick up the glass of water next to my bed.

I can't turn over or move in any type of way, and I'm urinating on myself. I say to the Lord, "Please don't let me die here. No one in my family knows that I'm sick."

Finally, after twenty-one days of feeling like I was on death's bed, I start recovering. My strength is back, and my chest doesn't feel like it's going to explode when I breathe. Thank you, Jesus. Thank you so much, Lord. I was so scared because I really thought that I was going to die here, alone.

I'm back at the barracks, and my drill instructor hands me some unexpected mail. It's a letter from Sarah, and I'm excited because no one has ever written me before. I'm reading the letter, and it starts off with the usual how-are-you-doing stuff. As I continue to read, she says that she is pregnant and that the baby is due within a few months.

Oh shit, my heart starts beating faster and my forehead starts sweating. I'm freaking nervous. This is definitely a big surprise for me, but I trust Sarah and I know that I was the only person intimate with her. Shit, it took me four months to get to know Sarah, so I know for a fact that she is not an easy, fast girl. Wow, I have a kid on the way, and I'm going to be a daddy.

The drill instructor allows me to resume my place with the same class despite my absence for thirty days. He says, "Lovett, you are an exceptional soldier and I have full confidence that you will excel to the top of this class." He was right because a couple of days later, I qualified first place with the M-16 assault rifle. I hit seventy-six targets out of eighty from a range of twenty-five to three hundred meters.

I am the tough guy in this unit; everybody respects me, including the drill instructor. I guess that's why he picked me to watch Nolan, who is on suicide watch. Nolan wants to get out of the army and go home by any means necessary.

He asked me to break his leg with a two-by-four, and I granted him his wish. I picked up a piece of wood, and when he closed his eyes, *whack!* I broke his leg. He screamed and cried from the pain. Damn, I know that hurt him.

Ironically, the drill instructor placed him on suicide watch, and I've been assigned to watch this fool. The drill instructor has no idea that I am the one who inflicted the injury to Nolan. "This guy really wants out of the army," I say to myself as I look at him endure the pain.

There is no way in hell that I would allow someone to hit me with a two-by-four-inch piece of wood. I guess it's worth it to him because he's going home in two days, and he keeps on saying, "Thank you, Sergio, thank you."

Finally, after weeks of training in these severe weather conditions, I graduate from basic training. I have been given a weekend pass to leave the military base for the first time, and I'm going straight to the club to party. Every guy here has the same agenda tonight, which is to find a nice girl and get laid.

Unfortunately, I haven't gotten lucky enough to hook up with a girl, and the night is almost over. Nevertheless, I am enjoying myself at the club just by merely being in the presence of females. I damn near forgot about the world outside the army.

These crackers have been drilling me intensely for weeks on end. They have tested me physically, intellectually, and emotionally; moreover, they have taught me how to kill and not be killed.

The weekend is over, and today I start training for my field, which is track and wheel motor-vehicle mechanic. That's a sixty-three Charlie in military terminology. The classes are a lot easier than the training, and the first thing that they're going to teach me is how to drive. I must learn how to drive everything, from a jeep to a tank, before they teach me how to repair it.

Months later I'm standing in front of a high-ranking officer, receiving my diploma. I couldn't be happier right now. I'm finished with all the training and classes. Tomorrow I'll be on an airplane headed back to Atlanta, and once I get there, I'm going straight to the Dale to see my family. Mom is going to be proud of me for a change, I hope.

The flight was short, and here I am back in Atlanta again. My mom is here to pick me up from the airport, and she has someone in the car with her. As I get closer to the car, I can see the passenger. Oh shit, it's Stephanie. What a pleasant surprise; she is just what the doctor ordered. I haven't been with a female for months, and she knows this, so it's going to be on tonight.

I've been given a couple of days off before I am to report to my home post, which is in Fort Benning, Georgia. It is only a two- or three-hour drive away from Atlanta. I've come up with a plan to make myself some extra cash. I'm going to buy a half of a pound of weed and take it back to base with me. Once I feel comfortable enough and hook up with the right people, I'm going to sell this weed in dime-bag increments.

It doesn't take me long to find out who likes to party and who are the snitches in my battalion. I have quickly established myself as the weed man; my shit comes straight from Atlanta. The local weed can't compete with the quality of my shit. I'm not only selling weed to soldiers, but at night I'm serving these niggas in the street too.

I came up with a scam on hashish, and people just can't get enough of it. I mix two eggs with a can of sage seasoning, bake it up in the oven, slice it up into squares, and sell it for hash. It looks just like hash, it smells just like hash, it taste just like hash, but it won't get you high. I usually mix it up in a joint of my good weed in case someone wants to smoke it first. Once they taste and smell the aroma of the sage, it's a sure sell.

I concentrate on the hotels and motels mostly because every weekend, a new set of soldiers is released with a weekend pass. Ninety percent of them want girls and drugs because they have just finished basic training. They are so vulnerable, it's like taking candy from a baby.

Sometimes I walk away from there with so much money, I'm afraid that I may get robbed. So I keep a sawed-off double-barreled shotgun on the backseat and a .357 Magnum under my shirt.

I live two separate lives. By day I am the ideal soldier, but at night I take my hair out from under my hat and turn into a hustler. I have a room in the barracks on post as if I live there, but I also have an apartment off post that no one knows about.

If they knew about the apartment, they would be wondering how I pay for it on my salary. I only use the apartment for entertaining girls. I don't like to take them on post to the barracks.

I've been dating a girl named Nita that lives in Baker Village. She is without a doubt one of the prettiest girls in the area. Her mother is an Indian and her dad is black, so she has the features of both parents.

Every time I take her somewhere with me, she gets second looks from every guy that passes her by. Nita is so fine with her silky long jet-black hair. She has a perfect set of white teeth, and her eyes are more beautiful than a baby doll's.

The only thing that I dislike about Nita is that she is beginning to be a little possessive of me. She's questioning my whereabouts, and she knows that I'm a hustler by night. I'm out here in these streets trying to get money, not girls, but she keeps accusing me of cheating on her in the process.

Weeks go by and I'm conducting business as usual. It's a beautiful Saturday afternoon, and one of my partners is at my apartment with me just hanging out. *Knock, knock, knock.* "Hey, Sergio, somebody is at your door," Farmer says. I get to the door, and it is Nita and one of her girlfriends. She has never walked over here unexpectedly before, so I'm wondering what's going on with her.

I can tell that both of them have been smoking weed because they're acting very silly and laughing a lot. Nita starts to get rude and decides that she's going to be destructive in my crib, but I'm not having it. I ask her politely to leave, but she ignores me. She continues to sit in my crib, disrespecting me, and I'm getting angrier by the moment.

I slowly get up and walk over to her and say, "Are you going to leave, or do I have to put you out?"

"Put me out, nigga," she says, and I immediately grant her wish. I pick her up and head straight for the door while Farmer is holding it open for me. I slowly put her down outside my door and step back into the crib.

As I try to close my door, she simultaneously breaks the glass in the door with her arms by trying to stop me from closing it. Oh shit, she's screaming, and blood is everywhere from her arms up to her neck. Now I'm trying to calm her down and get her in the car so that I can take her to the hospital. She's refusing to let me help her, and now the neighbors are coming out to see what's going on.

Nita starts walking up the street with her clothes all blooded up, and this does not look good. I'm sure that the police will be pulling up to my place soon, so I get in my car and leave. I go straight to Nita's mother's house and explain to her what just happened. Surprisingly, she is not angry with me and blames her daughter. As I drive away, I'm thinking that maybe I should stop seeing Nita.

A couple of days pass by, and Nita invites me over to see her again. I'm a little reluctant, but I show up anyway. We talk about the scenario at my crib, and she takes full blame for what happened. Everything seems to be cool now, so she starts making sexual advances at me. As things progress, I find myself on the floor naked with her on top of me.

Out of nowhere, all of a sudden, there is a knife at my throat. The point of the blade is already piercing my skin. "Oh shit, what the hell are you doing?" I ask her. "Nigga, have you been cheating on me?" she asks.

"Oh no, baby, take that knife away from my throat and let's talk about this. Calm down, baby. Calm down," I tell her. "You know that I love only you." She starts crying and says, "I'm sorry, Sergio. I'm so sorry." After removing the knife from her hand, I immediately leave with no intentions of ever returning.

Days later, the army ships us out to Fort Drum, New York, for winter training. It's very cold here, and they want us to stay for forty-five days. We are out in the woods day and night, and there must be three feet of snow on the ground. The only thing that keeps me from going insane here in this environment is the fact that I brought two ounces of weed with me.

The commander warned us about trying to bring drugs along and said that there would be drug-sniffing dogs to sniff us before entering the plane. I couldn't imagine being in the freaking woods for forty-five days and nights without my shit. I double-bagged the weed and put it inside of a sack full of garlic. The dog didn't smell a thing, and now I'm the only one here that has weed.

Once a couple of guys found out that I was holding, the sales began. I am selling this weed one joint at a time for five dollars a pop. These fools have no problem with paying my inflated price, considering where we are at and the conditions. Furthermore, I'm the one that took the risk. If the dog had sniffed me out, then I would be locked up in jail somewhere.

I am the man out here in these woods; everybody is looking for Lovett. After the troops finish their duties for the day, I'm the only source for entertainment. Paratroopers from the Eighty-Second Airborne out of North Carolina are dropping out of the sky from miles away. They are here to fight against us in a simulated war.

It's three o'clock in the morning and we are forming a convoy to move out on a mission. We can only use infrared lights for guidance through the woods, and we must stay close to the vehicle in front of us in order to see where we're going. After driving for two and a half hours, we finally come to a stop. I am so sleepy and tired from straining my eyes to see the vehicle in front of me, so I doze off.

When I awake, it is daylight and everyone is gone. Oh shit, I'm out here all alone. I'm driving a Goer, and it is the largest wheel-based vehicle in the army. The tires are six feet tall, and the vehicle is nothing short of a monster. It is loaded with simulation ammo, and if I get captured by the enemy, my company is going to be in trouble, big trouble.

I pull out my compass to navigate where I am, opposed to where I should be. I then reach in the back of the truck and grab a box of hand grenades to defend myself from the enemy. After driving about two miles, I run into an ambush.

The enemy placed a big log in the road in an effort to stop me from going through. I throw hand grenades left and right from the vehicle and drive it right over the log. The enemy soldiers are stunned by the grenades and baffled by my driving skills. I blew them away and drove right through them.

Farther down the road, I look over a hill to my right, and damn, I can't believe it; it's a freaking store. It's an old country store out in the boonies, and to my surprise, it is open. I pull up in the Goer, and people are looking at me strangely.

I walk inside and buy all the cookies, chips, and beer that they have on hand. These are hot commodities out there in the woods. We only have C rations, which are prepackaged military food.

Finally, after navigating and driving for hours, I find my company. The sergeant says, "Damn, Lovett, I thought that you had been captured. How in the hell did you make it back here?"

"Determination, Sergeant, that's how I made it back. Not only did I make it back, but I brought something for you."

"What is it, Lovett?" he asks as he looks at me inquisitively.

"Just a little taste of home, Sergeant, just a little taste of home," I say to him as I pass him a six-pack of Budweiser. "Where in the hell did you get this from?" he asks. "I found a store about five miles out from here, and I bought all the beer that they had," I reply. "You better keep this on the down low," he says. "I wouldn't want the captain to find out about this. You got it, Sergeant, you got it," I reply.

As he begins to walk away, he stops, turns around smiling, and says, "You can give me one of those joints too while you're at it. Damn, Lovett, you're the dope boy, you're the bootlegger, and with all those snacks, I see that you're going to be the freaking candy man too." I pass him a joint and look at him straight in the eyes and say, "Hey, man, Uncle Sam is not paying me enough to be out here in this shit."

Later that night, I'm called out to pull guard duty. As if it wasn't cold enough already inside the tent, now I have to stand in a foxhole, which is six feet deep, all night. While everyone else sleeps, three other soldiers and I take turns on guard in two different holes.

It is pitch-black dark, and I can only see twenty feet in front of me. Oh shit, a freaking Bobcat just walked right by me. Damn, I'm glad it didn't fall in this hole with me. Man, I'll be glad when this little war game is over.

After forty-five days and nights, we finally leave the boonies of New York and arrive back in Fort Benning, Georgia. I went all the way to New York and never got a chance to see a single building. We all have four days off, so I'm going to drive to Florida so that I can see Sarah and the baby.

It's a boy, and she named him Trey. I'm a little pissed at the fact that she didn't give him my last name, but I'm not going to make a big fuss about it.

I arrive in Florida, and as soon as Sarah sees me, she jumps up into my arms. "Hey, baby, I miss you so much, Sergio," she says. "I miss you too, girl, so where is the baby?" I ask. "He's in the bedroom, asleep," she says. "Then wake his little ass up," I reply. She wakes him up and hands him over to me. I look at him and say, "Damn, he looks just like me."

I spent the entire weekend with Sarah and the baby, and we really enjoyed each other. She still loves me and wants us to be a family, but I don't think I'm ready to be a family man yet. I'm back at my apartment off post, I'm here all alone, and I like it that way. I don't have to answer to anyone, and I don't have to argue with anyone.

Months go by and I decide to trade my Mustang for a Thunderbird. It's white with a white vinyl top and white leather interior. This car is superclean, and it makes me feel like Super Fly. I've never had much of a problem with getting girls, but this car is a babe magnet.

Some of the local dope boys are starting to get jealous of me. I have been selling weed on their turf at night and getting too much attention from their girls. The only reason that they haven't tried to rob me is because they know that I have a .357 Magnum tucked under my shirt.

Years pass, and what do you know, shit, it's time for me to get out of the army. I have served my time, and now they want me to reenlist. There is no way in hell that I would put up with this shit another three years, so I'm going to make my rounds and get the hell out of here. I am no longer the property of the United States Army. I'm a freeman now; damn, it feels like I've been born again.

Red

Finally, I'm back in the city of Atlanta, and it feels so good to be home. I'm riding around the city in my big white Thunderbird with a pocket full of money and a .357 Magnum tucked away under my shirt. I never look for trouble, but I like to be ready if trouble finds me.

Tonight I am on my way to a party that's being held at the Knights of Columbia off Candler Road. I was invited by a friend of a friend, so I have no idea who the host is. It takes me five minutes to find a parking space because the crowd is hanging out in the parking lot.

Wow, the females here outnumber the guys, and these girls are looking fabulous. There is one girl in particular that has been watching my every move, and she's very pretty. We make eye contact several times before I get enough courage to ask her to dance.

She accepts my invitation to the dance floor, and it is love at first sight. Damn, she is so pretty with those little freckles on her cheek. She has a tremendous smile and a perfect body. This girl should be a model because she has all the right features. She says her name is Loretta, but everyone calls her Red. She doesn't hesitate to give me her phone number following the dance.

With number in hand, I head back to the car, feeling that my mission has been accomplished for the night. I got a phone number and a dance from the finest girl at the party. I can't wait until tomorrow comes so that I can call her up. I think that she was just as excited about me as I was about her.

The next day I find myself knocking on her door to pick her up for dinner, and she's more beautiful now than she was last night. Thank you, Jesus. Thank you, Lord. She is so fine, and I'm definitely going to make her mine. After dinner, we park the car on Peachtree Street and take a nice, long walk while we converse with each other.

It's magic off the rip. Red and I have some serious chemistry going on. The first kiss is slow and tender, but it seems to last for an eternity. I want her so bad right now, and in her eyes I can see that she feels the same.

This is the first date, so I am definitely not going to go there. I don't want her to feel disrespected. As I look into her beautiful big eyes, before I depart, my spirit tells me that she is going to love me and I am going to love her back.

Months later, Red and I are in a serious relationship. I see only her, and she fulfills my every need. We both are in love with each other, and we never let a day go by without calling or seeing each other. Life is good right now for me, and I'm happy. I have a beautiful girlfriend, a good job, and I'm putting together a band.

The band is merely just my two brothers and I messing around. Rob plays the drums, Donald plays the guitar, and I play the bass guitar. Together we call ourselves the Brothers Three Band. We have only been playing together for a few months, and the sound is starting to get very tight.

Between Red, work, and the band rehearsals, I stay on the go most of the time. I have a serious passion for music, and I spend a lot of money on equipment. I'm trying to build up enough equipment to do live performances. I think about the band all day long while I'm working. I have visions of myself onstage in front of crowds of people enjoying the music.

Red and I decide to move in to an apartment together on Campbellton Road. It's on the southwest side of the city, and both of us are from the east side. Red's family lives in Decatur, and I'm from the Dale. I like the southwest area because business on Campbellton Road is booming. The finest nightclub in this city for blacks is Mr. V's Figure 8, and it is literally two blocks away from my crib.

Actually there are four nightclubs located on this street, so every weekend, this area is cluttered with traffic. Campbellton Road is one of the best streets in this city for black business, and I'm right here in the midst of it all. I work across the street from my apartment at a Buick dealership as an auto technician, and the pay is great. It enables me to take good care of my little family.

Red has two beautiful little girls, Tony and Keesha. I love both of them, and they feel the same way about me. Keesha, the younger of the two, follows me around all night like a shadow. She has just simply melted my heart.

I probably spend more time with her than I do with her mother. She can get just about anything that she wants from me, and she knows it too. I have spoiled her rotten, and she loves every minute spent with me.

A year passes, and the band has grown to six members. We now have a keyboard player, a lead guitarist, and a lead vocalist. We changed our name to Positive Force and hired a tailor to make our outfits. All our outfits usually have the same color scheme, but we all choose different styles.

We have a booking agent that keeps us pretty busy every weekend. He books us on local and out-of-state gigs, from Florida all the way up to Canada. Music is my bread and butter now. My brothers and I decided to quit our jobs and just play nightclubs two or three nights per week.

It's a lot of work involved with putting together a show that will please an audience. Somehow, I became the one in charge of the image of the band.

Red is working for a modeling agency, and she does shows on the weekend also. We take the kids over to her mother's place when both of us have to work the same weekend. I have seen a couple of her shows, and she is very good at modeling. She can make any designer's clothing look good.

Our booking agent called us with a gig in Canada for thirty days, and we're all very excited about it. This is going to be the longest trip that we have taken by far. We usually rent a truck for our local gigs, but this time we need a van and a trailer. We pool all our resources together and come up with the money for the van. I tune up the engine, change the oil, and have all the tires replaced with new ones.

We rent the trailer as a one-day local, but we have no intentions on ever bringing it back. The six of us pray together, load up, and hit the road, heading for Canada. Suzanne is our new lead vocalist, and I'm surprised that her boyfriend let her leave with us.

Jimmy is our new keyboard player, and he recently moved from New Jersey. Reggie, our roadie, is going along with us to drive, move equipment, work the lighting system and sound board. He's from Trinidad, and he is a very funny guy; he keeps us laughing all the time.

As we get farther and farther away from home and closer to Canada, the van starts giving us problems. There is a serious exhaust system leak, and the fumes are entering inside the van. Everyone is sick with extreme headaches, and Suzanne is about to pass out.

I have been driving for hours with my head halfway outside the window so that I can get some fresh air. Unfortunately, everyone else in the back of the van is getting most of the fumes.

The van is also having a difficult time going up the slopes of these snowy hills. I have to drive in a snake pattern in order to get enough traction to make it to the top of the hill. Everyone is praying that the van doesn't stop moving forward, because once it stops, there is a big possibility that it will slide back down the hill.

Slowly but surely we make it to the top of the last big hill in sight. I pull over to the side of the road to stop and thank God in prayer for getting us to the top of the hills during the snowstorm. As soon as Suzanne stepped out of the van and got a whiff of the fresh air, *bam!* She passes out. She falls to the ground and begins to slide down the hill but I grab her by her coat in just the nick of time.

She would've ended up at the bottom of a two-hundred-foot drop if I hadn't grabbed her. I literally saved her life, and everyone is praising God because that was a scary, close call. We sit inside the van for an hour without the engine running to get relief from the fumes for a while, and it is freezing cold.

No one wants to help me out with the driving, not even Reggie, and this is supposed to be his job. We have been arguing all the way up the road for days because they refuse to drive. When I get tired, I pull over and sleep for an hour, and no one volunteers to take over the wheel.

After a couple of days and nights, I finally reach our destination in Canada. Wow, it is so beautiful here; the mountains are covered in snow, and the lakes are frozen like a piece of ice. Our employer gives us the keys to two cottages and the nightclub. We get to eat anything on the menu at the restaurant three times a day. We have full access to the club and bar so that we can rehearse whenever we want to.

This is going to be a sweet little gig. We only have to play Thursday night through Saturday night, and Sunday through Wednesday, we just chill out doing whatever we want to do. They also have a television advertisement of us performing at the club, so when we walk around the city, people recognize us.

It's a great feeling to be admired and appreciated for something that I love to do. I can't begin to explain how I feel when we are standing in front of a crowd of people waiting to see our performance. I always have butterflies in my stomach up until we hit the first note, then it's no shame in my game. I'm a little bit shy when I am off the stage, but when I'm performing, it's another world for me.

We were extremely lucky to make it across the border with an ounce of weed, but here they smoke hashish. The squares of hashish are stamped with Rolls Royce symbols, and it is the highest quality available. It is so potent that we can only smoke one joint before performance, and it's six of us. If we were smoking weed, we would have to smoke four joints to get the same high.

We're living like rock stars, eating well, drinking well, smoking well, and partying with all the French-speaking girls that we can handle. Every weekend I get a new girlfriend, and they are absolutely beautiful. I'm slowly starting to understand and speak French, being that it is the primary language here.

A club owner from another city came out to see us perform, and he was very impressed with our show. He wants us to perform at his place when we finish here, so our agent back in Atlanta has booked us to play in Boston for two weeks because of the time overlap. So the plan is for us to leave here and go to Boston for two weeks then return to Canada to play at another location.

After four months of partying at this ski resort every weekend, the time comes for us to leave and head back to the States. Leaving is bittersweet for me because I was getting accustomed to the lifestyle.

I could live here forever, but everyone else is homesick. Sure, I miss Red and I want to see her, but this is what I love to do. So if I have to stay on the road to get paid, then so be it; I have no problem with that.

We arrive in Boston and find the club in an area called Dorchester. As we unload the equipment from the trailer, some strange guy tries to steal from us, but we catch him before he enters the trailer. We have to be very careful now because we are back in the hood. We haven't been around other blacks for four months. There were only whites at the resort in Canada, and they didn't try to steal from us.

After setting up the equipment and doing a sound check, we leave the club to find a couple of rooms at a hotel downtown. Once we get settled in and cleaned up, it's smoke time. We never consume much alcohol before a show; that's one of our rules. We just sit around and smoke weed while we discuss the show, song by song.

The sun goes down and I'm walking around the room, saying, "It is showtime, baby. It is showtime." I try to keep everyone hyped up and in good spirit before we hit the stage so that we can enjoy ourselves as we perform together.

The parking lot at the club is full when we arrive, and that is always a good sign. Once we enter the door, all eyes are on us as we hit the stage and crank things up. The first couple of rows of tables are women only, and they are excited to see us. My brother Donald and I have cordless guitars, so we approach the tables and tease the girls as we play and dance.

It turned out to be a very fun night. We were tight on every song that we played, and the crowd enjoyed themselves. As we exit the club to go back to the hotel, we are approached by a couple of girls that want to have an after-party with us.

When we opened the door of the van, to our surprise, there are more girls already sitting inside of the van, waiting for us. They all smile, and one of them says to us, "We're following you guys to the hotel."

It's three o'clock in the morning, and we plan on partying till daylight with these girls. As soon as the girls get into our rooms, they start choosing whom they want to be with, and it's like spin the freaking bottle for sex up in here. We keep a box of protection just for occasions like this one, because there are always groupies in every city.

After partying in Boston for two weeks, we find ourselves back at the Canadian border, under search. Reggie was able to get in the last time, but this time they will not let him enter without a green card. He is from Trinidad, and he doesn't have the correct paperwork. They have pulled all of our equipment out of the trailer and searched it for drugs. The weed is hidden inside the three keyboards, so they will never find it.

Unfortunately, they will not let Reggie pass, so we give him enough money to make it back home to Atlanta. It's sad, and it seems unfair, but the show must go on, so we roll out to Canada. The last time we were here, we were near Montreal. This time we are going to Ottawa, and I'm all excited again.

We finally arrive at our destination, and it is a huge hotel. We set up all the equipment and do a sound check before retiring to our rooms. The guys are starting to get burned out with the traveling and working. They are starting to whine about missing their girlfriends at home, so I know that after this job is finished, we're going back to Atlanta.

The thirty days in Ottawa come to pass quickly; before you know it, we are back in Atlanta. Red is so happy to see me, and I feel the same about her. I missed her as well, even though I could've stayed longer. Everyone in the Dale is talking about our road trip to Canada and anticipates seeing us perform here in Atlanta.

Right now, we just want to spend time with our girlfriends and family, so we're going to take a couple of weeks off before we perform again. Our booking agent has already set up gigs for Club VIP, Club Sansusi, and Mr. V's Figure 8. All of them are nice nightclubs that carry a big crowd.

Red and I make each other happy, and we are still very much in love with each other. I spend as much time as possible with her and the kids. My lease is up on the apartment at Deerfield on Campbellton Road, so I've decided to move back on the east side to Snapfinger Woods. It is a nice, quiet area surrounded by a golf course, ponds, and trees.

I rented a three-bedroom apartment this time so that the girls can have their own rooms. It is a very nice place. Red and the kids love it. I went back to work full-time because the band decided not to go out of state anymore on gigs. Everyone is back on the job force, and we now only do local gigs within a hundred-mile radius.

Years pass and everything is going well, Red and I are still together, and the band is working every weekend. We have groupies that follow us around from one club to another every weekend. I finally got rid of the Thunderbird and bought a BMW, but before I drive it, I'm going to have it customized.

I purchased a front spoiler, a rear spoiler, and a side ground effects package for it. I'm having the spoiler kit installed before the car gets painted. I picked a very odd color. It's a mixture between burnt orange and copper, with metal flakes and clear pearl coating. The car is going to be awesome when it's finished, and I can barely wait.

Over the years I have become a very good dresser. I've spent a lot of money on my wardrobe. I have an image to maintain on and off stage, and I like the finer things in life. Don't get it twisted because you can still find me hanging out in some of the roughest and toughest places in the city, but I do prefer the high life.

I finally picked up my BMW today, and it is prettier than I expected it to be. The paint is so shiny that it looks as if it were still wet. I've been getting compliments at every stop that I make, and everyone loves the color.

I have the rims painted in the same color as the car, and it has a serious European look, no chrome, baby, just paint. The spoiler package makes the car appear to be low to the ground, which gives it a fast, sporty look. The car is tight work.

Months later, Red and I are starting to have some serious issues going on with each other. We don't trust each other anymore, and it's causing us to argue a lot. She's insecure from the attention that I get from women, and I'm insecure from the attention she gets from men. We both are entertainers, so what do we do?

I am definitely not going to stop performing because of her, and I don't expect her to stop modeling for me either. I was all right until her modeling group had a meeting at our place one night. After the meeting, I overheard one of the male models say, "Pull out the porno tape and let's have a party." I couldn't believe my ears; did this punk-ass nigga just disrespect me in my own house?

I went straight back down the hallway to our bedroom, into the closet, and grabbed my pistol. As I entered the family room, where the meeting was being held, I chambered a round. *Click, click,* the sound of the bullet being injected into the chamber was heard by everyone.

When they turned and looked at me, I was standing there with a .45-caliber pistol in my hand. I looked at the guy that made the porno remark and said, "You got five seconds to get the fuck out of my house."

Things have not been the same since that event. I don't feel comfortable with her changing clothes in front of guys anymore. I was standing in the audience at her last show, and when she came down the runway, the guy next to me made a very nasty remark concerning her. He had no idea that she was my girlfriend, so he and his buddy kept talking away. I never mentioned anything about it to Red. I just kept it to myself.

Today the both of us are at our mother's place. I'm just sitting around talking to my mom, and then the phone rings. It's Red and she's crying, telling me to turn on the television for the news. She says that there is a fire in our complex, and the unit that's on fire looks just like ours. "Calm down, baby. Calm down. There are fifty units in that complex. Chances are it is not ours," I tell her.

She and I had previously planned to spend the night with our parents this Sunday, so we don't go to back to our complex. The following day, I receive a call at work from the property manager of my complex. She says, "Mr. Lovett, I have been trying to get in contact with you because there was a fire in the complex last night and your unit has some minor smoke damage. The Red

Cross has also been trying to reach you for any assistance that you may need. I think that you should come right away, Mr. Lovett, so that we can assist you with your living arrangement." I didn't say a word back to her. I just hung up the phone. I leave my job and pick Red up on the way. "I told you, Sergio. I told you that it was our place," she says to me with tears in her eyes.

Oh shit, the freaking place is burned to the ground. Why would she tell me it was only minor smoke damage? Everything is burned—furniture, clothing, electronics, personal items that can never be replaced are all gone. Red is hysterical, and I'm doing my best to be strong for her. She has lost all her kids' clothing, her clothes, and all her personal shit; it's just a big mess.

The manager says that kids were playing with firecrackers, being that yesterday was the Fourth of July, and accidently started a fire on the side of our unit. She offers us a different apartment, but we decline because we don't have anything to put in it. Besides that, she is expecting me to pay rent in one week. "Are you freaking kidding me?" I ask. "Hell no, I'm not paying you rent next week."

I move back in with my mom, and Red moves into one of her girlfriends' home. We still see each other, but things aren't the same and I can sense it. I have a gut feeling that she is seeing someone else, and sooner or later it will come to the light.

Rob and I are at the gas station, fueling up before we head off to practice. I'm sitting in the passenger seat when all of a sudden, this fine-ass girl hops out of her car and goes inside. "Damn, Rob, did you see that? She is so fine." As soon as she came back to her car, I introduced myself and gave her my phone number. She said that her name is Strawberry and that she would call me later.

Damn, I haven't been this excited about a girl since I met Red. Strawberry called me, and I'm on my way to see her at her crib in Clarkston. She opens the door to let me in and greets me with a hug. Wow, she's holding on to me pretty tight for this to be our first encounter. I think she likes me, and she has no problem with showing it.

Weeks go by, and I have been sneaking around to see Strawberry every chance I get. I told Strawberry all about my girlfriend, Red, and she is still interested in seeing me. So I'm going back and forth from Red to Strawberry, from Strawberry to Red. My instincts are starting to tell me that Red is hiding something from me, so I'm going to pop up on her unannounced.

When I get to the street of Red's friend's house, I notice a strange car parked in the driveway. I shut off the engine and the headlights to my BMW and coast into the yard. As I walk by the strange car, I place my hand on the grill to feel how hot it is. The heat from the grill tells me that the car had not been parked very long.

When I get to the door, I notice that the curtains are not closed completely, so I take a peek inside the house. Oh shit, Red is sitting on the couch next to a guy with her nightgown on. I'm shaking from anger, but I must control it before I knock on the door. I walk back to my car and grab the .45. I put the pistol under my shirt and slowly proceed to knock on the door.

I'm still peeking in the window as she peeks out. "Oh my god, it is Sergio," she says. She tells the guy to go into the other room with her sister who is visiting and pretend that he is there to see her. I can hear and see everything that they are doing, but she doesn't realize it. I knock on the door, and she opens it looking as if she just seen a freaking ghost.

"What's up, baby? How are you doing tonight?" I ask her. "I'm doing all right," she says as she darts into the bathroom. I immediately walk into the family room, where the guy is sitting next to her sister, and introduce myself. This fool has the audacity to have a smile on his face as if I'm a joke.

Click, click, the .45 is out and I just chambered a round. Everyone in the room scatters outside except him, because I have the pistol pointing right at him. "Do you think this shit is funny now, nigga, and do I look like a freaking joke to you?"

"No, sir, Mr. Sergio, no, sir, please don't shoot me," he says. "You got five seconds to get the hell out of here, or else I'm going to put a cap in your ass," I reply.

Red has locked herself in the bathroom, and she's screaming, "Please don't kill him, Sergio. Please don't kill him!" As he gets up and walks quickly toward the door, I can't resist planting my foot right in the crack of his ass. He runs to his car, scared as hell, and peels out of the driveway.

I put the pistol back up under my shirt, and Red finally cracks the door open to see what's going on. I snatch her pretty little ass out of the bathroom, and she says, "I'm sorry, Sergio. He is only just a friend." I really don't want to hear anything she has to say, so I just give her a disgusted look and walk away. As I drive away, I know that the relationship between Red and I is over.

I drive straight to Strawberry's crib, and immediately she knows that something is wrong. I'm trying my best to maintain my composure, but she drills it out of me anyway. The truth is what I tell her, and I literally pour my heart out because I am devastated about the fact of the matter. After listening to me tell her about the scenario, she looks me in the eye and says, "Sergio, you are in love with her."

She is absolutely right; even though I am lying next to her, I know in my heart that I'm still in love with Red. I'm sick, and Strawberry knows it. Instead of her getting an attitude with me about discussing Red, she feels my pain and comforts me. She pampers me and treats me like a king, and then she makes passionate love to me for the first time.

The next day, one of my old partners from the unit calls me up and says he's got a good lick for us to pull off. I'm like, "Well, what's up, man? What are you trying to do?" He says that he knows where the big dope boy's stash spot is and that he was going to take it. "There's an ounce of cocaine in this nigga's fuel door of his Mercedes Benz," he says. "Hell no, man, you know that I'm not into no shit like that," I tell him.

Sure enough, the next day, this nigga has an ounce of cocaine in his pocket. I've never indulged in the use of cocaine before, but tonight I am going to try it for the first time. Shortly after sniffing the cocaine, I'm starting to feel the effects of it. Damn, this is a totally different high compared to weed. I'm not in a happy, social mood. I feel reserved and paranoid.

Two days later, I find out that my partner is in the hospital. The owner of the Mercedes Benz tracked him down and paid some guys to bust him up real good. I rush to the hospital to visit him, and when I see him, I am speechless.

Damn, they beat the shit out of him. His arm is broken, his ribs are cracked, and his face is swollen beyond recognition. I am glad as hell that I didn't go with him, or the same would've happened to me.

The management at Snapfinger Woods Apartments called me back again to offer me another unit, and I accepted it. I guess I have to start all over again with furniture, because right now I don't so much as own a chair. Red has been trying to reconcile with me, and it's starting to work because I still love her. Strawberry, on the other hand, is on me like glue; she has fallen in love with me.

With her persistence and seductive nature, Red finally wins me back. I stupidly allow her to move back in with me, and hope for the best. Strawberry is not happy about the situation at all, but she still allows me to see her.

I think that she is truly in love with me, and I really should be with her instead of Red. My birthday is on July 19, and Strawberry's birthday is on July 18. We have a lot in common with each other, and our chemistry together is unbelievable.

Months pass and I'm going back and forth, forth and back between Red and Strawberry. Red called me at work today and informed that she and the kids would be staying at her mother's for the night. So I'm heading home to a quiet, empty place tonight. I'll be there all by myself.

As I open the door, I notice toilet tissue on the floor. At first I think that maybe one of the kids dropped it on their way out this morning. The tissue leads me from my front door, all the way upstairs to the bathroom in the master's room. Who in the hell would roll this paper out like this?

Red doesn't have a car, so how can this be? I know damn well this paper was not here when I locked my door this morning. I call and ask her anyway, and she says, "No, Sergio, I haven't been there." I hang up the phone and immediately grab my pistol.

Somebody has been in here, and they possibly may still be here. As soon as I chamber a round, I can hear strange noises coming from downstairs. It sounds like someone is moving around, and I think it's more than one person.

All kinds of thoughts are running through my mind at this point. I'm wondering if Red knows about Strawberry and trying to set me up. It's ironic for all this to be happening on the very night that she chooses to stay at her mother's. I don't trust her, and I don't put it past her. She is highly capable of orchestrating something like this.

I decide to take the bold approach and speak out because now I feel threatened. Loudly I say, "Whoever is inside this place, if you want me, then come upstairs and get me. I'm right here waiting for you, me and my .45." I wait a couple of seconds, and then I hear my front door open and close.

Damn, somebody was truly in here. This girl really tried to set me up. It's dark outside, and they may have tampered with my car, so I call Strawberry and she rushes over to pick me up like a trooper. I have to admit that Strawberry is always there when I need her.

Now I know for sure that Red and I are not going to make it. I could never truly trust her again. How can I be with a woman that I know wants to see me hurt? It will never be the same between the two of us. She has really crossed the line, trying to bring physical harm upon me. We are now at the point of no return, and I'll be moving my shit from here first thing tomorrow.

Strawberry

After having my stuff tucked away in a storage room for a month, I finally find a nice apartment in Stone Mountain. It's huge, and that's just the way I like it. I have my musical equipment all set up in one of the rooms, and now I can focus more on my second love, music.

God is my first love, and I really need to get back to him. It seems that as long as I'm not giving God any of my time, Satan doesn't attack me in my dreams as much. He doesn't ride my back anymore the way he did when I was a kid; now he torments me in my dreams.

I have the worst dreams imaginable, and in all my nightmares, I'm about to be killed. The dreams peak at the very moment before death, and I always seem to wake up suddenly before it happens. I wake up with my heart about to jump out of my chest from the rapid beating. I'm sweating as if someone poured a bucket of water over me, and I'm glad that it was only a dream.

If the dreams wake me up at three o'clock in the morning, then surely I will be up the rest of the night. I'm always afraid to go back to sleep. I would rather be tired than scared any day. The dreams are so realistic that my mind and soul are truly there in the midst of it. God shows me visions through dreams, but Satan shows me death.

Tonight the band is playing at the premier VIP club. It's a high-scale club located in Buckhead, one of the most exquisite areas of the city. The band is all hyped up, and we've anticipated playing here for a long time. The place is crawling with females because tonight the club has two different acts. After we perform for forty-five minutes, the male strippers come out onstage and really make the girls go crazy.

Strawberry usually comes to every show, but tonight I don't want her to be here. If she wants to see male strippers, then she is going to have to do that on her own time, not on mine. After the show, I go straight to her place, and she is still up waiting for me. This girl is so sweet, and I'm really starting to like her and her kids.

She has two daughters and a son. The boy is the youngest, and he is just a cute little three-year-old baby. The girls, however, are ten and thirteen. I have no problem with the girls whatsoever; we get along just fine. The baby, on the other hand, is pissed off at me because I'm getting some of his mother's attention. Just the other day, he called me a black mother; shut your mouth.

Months go by and all has been going well. Then out of the blue, Red starts calling me back again. She has been trying to get me to pick her up and bring her over to my place for a week now. Her persistence has overwhelmed me, and I find myself pulling up to my apartment with her in the car.

I'm a little nervous because I do not want Strawberry to see Red over here with me. I'm sure that she would really be pissed off at me this time, and I wouldn't blame her. She would have every right to be angry with me even though this is my place. I expect her to be straight with me, yet I'm doing something that I know she wouldn't like behind her back.

This doesn't feel right, and my spirit is telling me that Strawberry is going to pop up on me unannounced at any moment. Yet and still I have Red sitting here looking all sexy and hot with her tight ripped jeans on. She is trying her best to seduce me. No sooner than she reaches over to kiss me, we are interrupted by a knock on the door.

I get up and look into the peephole. Oh shit, it's Strawberry. I am definitely not going to open the door, so I'll just pretend that I'm not at home. Red is not saying a word because she knows that I have been seeing someone else. We move to the bedroom in order to get farther away from the door. This way, Strawberry can't hear us talking.

As we're sitting in the bedroom, the knocking stops, so I assume that Strawberry is gone. Then all of a sudden, the next thing I hear is something hitting my window, and my apartment is three floors up from the ground.

I look out the window, and Strawberry is standing there below my window, looking up at me. I'm busted, and there is no excuse that I can give her later. Damn, I know that she's hurt and feels betrayed, and I feel terrible about that.

Days pass before she finally answers my phone call. All I can do at this point is show her that I'm man enough to admit what I did was wrong. I definitely don't want to insult her intelligence by telling a lie. So I tell her the truth about why I wouldn't answer my door, and then I apologize to her. I'll give her a couple of days and she will be all right.

The next day we have a band meeting, and I bring up the same topic that I always do, and that's saving money. We have been playing these nightclubs for years now and don't have a damn thing to show for it, except our personal equipment.

When we get paid, I always suggest that we take some money off the top for savings before we pay out. Once we split the money up, getting these niggas to pay dues is like pulling teeth.

I want to record original music in the studio, but they are content with just playing copy material. My vision is clearly different from theirs, and I'm starting to get frustrated with their way of thinking.

If I have to do it all by myself, then so be it, but I am surely going to record my own music in the studio. One day they are going to hear it on the radio. God has shown me visions of this over and over.

Every time we play in a nightclub, we have to do two forty-five-minute shows. Each show consists of seven songs, and out of those songs, only one of them is an original. I have been suggesting that we play two original songs per show, but they don't like that idea either.

I'm starting to feel as if they don't want my shit to get any exposure, being that I write most of the original songs. Not only that, but I sing most of them too. We have hired and fired four different lead singers because I was not happy with their performance.

Sure, they can sing, but none of them are performers. They really don't know how to work the crowd and interact with them. My brother Donald and I always have to do it for them.

I'm looking for someone who can sing, dance, and talk to the crowd between songs. The lead singer is supposed to direct the band and take charge onstage, not sing and freeze up. We play funk music, and I refuse to play behind someone that is not better than me.

I guess that I'm going to have to do the studio project all by myself, and that's cool too. When we are at rehearsals, they seldom want to spend any time on original material. They don't realize that we can play copy material for ten more years and it's still not going to make us successful. The only thing that is going to do that is a hit song; that's why when I'm alone, I write and compose my own shit.

It's been four days since I spoke to Strawberry; finally, today she called. She wants to come over to my place tonight and have a discussion with me about our future together, if, in fact, we still have one. I actually miss her a lot, so I know that I do have strong feelings for her. Depending on what she says, maybe I'll get my act together and do right by her.

When Strawberry steps in the door, I have everything just right for her. I have prepared her favorite dishes, which are T-bone steaks, lobster tails, baked potatoes, and a salad. I have a big bottle of Crown Royal for drinks and Kenny G. playing on the stereo with a room full of candles.

The candles lead down the hallway to my bedroom, and it's lit up like a Christmas tree all around my bed. Before the talking begins, I take her by the hand and lead her straight to the bedroom. We look into each other's eyes as the light from the candles creates sparkles in them. Finally, she kisses me and submits herself to me.

As we lie next to each other afterward, she tells me that she is pregnant and that she wants to move in with me. I'm totally surprised and caught off guard, but I do love the idea of having a baby. I screwed up the opportunity to raise my son, so maybe the Lord is giving me a second chance.

I hope that the baby is a girl because I have always wanted a daughter to spoil rotten. We love each other, so why not move in together and live as a family? She and I both can save a little money in the process, being that we both like the finer things in life.

Months pass and everything is all good between Strawberry and I. We are really enjoying each other. We do a lot of shopping, and she has great taste in everything. Before you know it, the entire crib is laid out with exquisite furniture and decor. We are doing pretty damn good right now, and we don't lack anything.

I have also grown quite fond of Strawberry's family. Sometimes on Sundays we go to her grandmother's house for dinner. I always have a wonderful time when I go over there. Everybody calls her grandmother by her nickname, which is Nanny. Living in the house with her is Strawberry's mother Dottie, her cousin Cola, and Cola's daughter, Brianna.

There are too many females in this house. The little boy and I are the only male species here. They all spoil me and treat me like a king; it's unbelievable. They even get an attitude with Strawberry if she doesn't fix my plate and serve it to me. I seem to have the seal of approval from each and every one of them, and Strawberry knows it.

I have been putting my face against Strawberry's stomach every day since the first day that she told me that she was pregnant. I usually sing or hum to the baby so that she can feel my vibrations. Today something is different when I put my face up against Strawberry's stomach. I can sense that something is inside with the baby.

It makes me feel so uneasy that I mention it to Strawberry. I look at her and say, "I don't know what it is, but there is something inside of the sack with the baby." She looks at me as if I'm crazy and says, "I am five and a half months pregnant, so why would you say something like that to me, Sergio?"

"I'm sorry, Strawberry," I reply. "I don't mean to get you worried or upset. It's just that I know that something is inside of the sack with the baby, and maybe it will be a good idea to go to the doctor and find out what it is."

"What are you, a freaking human x-ray machine or something, Sergio?" she replies with a sarcastic attitude. I decide to leave it alone because I don't want her to get upset.

The next day we go to visit her dad. He lives only fifteen minutes away from her granny's place, and I spend a lot of time with him as well. He is a very nice guy, and he will do anything for Strawberry and her sister Jackie. I get along well with him, but it is something about his spirit that does not sit well with me. I never say anything to Strawberry about it, but I feel dark energy present around him.

Strawberry's dad is very funny, and he definitely knows how to entertain people. He's an old man, but he loves to dance with young girls, very young girls. He can dance quite well for his age, and he always shows off at the little family gatherings. Sometimes when I look at him, I see negative forces all around him. I feel that at some point and time, he has been involved with voodoo or something of that nature.

I would never discuss this with Strawberry because I'm sure that she will naturally defend her dad. It may very well be something that she has no clue about, but my spirit rarely misleads me. Her dad tried to get me to play a spiritual game with him that consists of a board with astrological charts and the use of spiritual energy. Don't get it twisted because I really do like her dad; it's his spirit that I don't like.

A couple of days later, Strawberry decides to go to the doctor for a routine checkup. I'm at work when she calls me, crying her heart out. "Sergio, Sergio, oh no, Sergio, I've lost the baby! I've lost the baby, Sergio!" Strawberry is devastated, and I know that she needs me right now, so I encourage her to calm down because I am on my way to her.

When I get home to her, she has her face hidden from me under the bed covers. She is so hurt and disappointed, and I can feel her pain as I begin to cry along with her. Softly she says, "You were right about something inside the sack with the baby. It was a fibroid tumor, and it erupted inside the sack and killed the baby." I do everything that I can possibly do to comfort her for the next few days, hoping that she will be just fine.

A week later, I get a telephone call from one of my old partners. He wants me to help him pull off a lick. He works with a guy from Bogotá, Colombia. The guy went home on vacation and brought back four ounces of cocaine to sell, so he wants to rob him. He wants me to pretend to be the buyer and then pull my gun out on the both of them.

We pick up the dude on the corner of a major street downtown. I'm already positioned in the backseat, and he jumps in the front. My partner introduces me as Jimmy from South Carolina, and we are supposed to be old friends. As soon as the dude passed the bags of cocaine to me for inspection, *click, click.* I chambered a round into my .45.

Instead of pointing the gun at the white boy, I put it to the head of my partner. That really scared the shit out of him. I told him that if he wanted to live, it would be a good idea for him to get his ass out at the next red light. Oh shit, this dude is getting out before the car even stops.

After the dude got out and we turned the corner, we knew that we were home free. My partner looks at me and says, "Damn, nigga, I didn't know that you were going to pull your shit out on me. I knew what was going on, but you still scared the hell out of me, Sergio. You had this crazy look in your eyes that fooled even me, and I'm the one that set this shit up," he says.

"Hey, man, you told me that you work with this guy, so I had to make it look good. You wouldn't want him to think that you set him up, so that's why I put the gun in your face instead of his. Hell, he was scared for you. He probably think that you're going to end up dead somewhere," I tell him.

"I guess you're right," he says. "But yet and still, you were quite convincing, Sergio." So we get back to his crib and make an even split, two ounces of raw cocaine each. This shit is so potent that I'm afraid to sell or use it as it is. After we put a little cut on it to tone it down for snorting, I begin to start packaging it so that I can get paid.

As I'm bagging up the packages, my spirit tells me that this is going to come back to haunt me someday. I should have never done what I just did. Someone could've been injured or killed, and I would've been completely responsible.

Thank you, Jesus. Thank you, Lord, for allowing everyone to walk away unharmed. I promise that I will never do anything like this again. Forgive me, Lord. As I look at the cocaine on the table, reality sets in, and I'm ashamed of what I've done.

It doesn't take long before I start getting a substantial number of customers. The quality of the package that we have is the talk of the neighborhood. We have the fire, and everybody that gets high in this neighborhood is looking for it.

I have been pinching a few bags of cocaine for my own, personal use. I use it with friends and certain girls that I run into from time to time. It's getting to be a habit that I do every weekend, and it's starting to cost me money.

Strawberry knows that I am getting high on the weekends, but she never says anything about it. I only do a little portion at a time because I have to remain functional around my customers and family.

Months later we have another band meeting. I surprise everyone by announcing that I no longer want to do the nightclub scene. After ten years of playing together, I feel that none of them are willing to invest their money into recording original music in the studio.

It is a bittersweet moment, but it is something that I have to do. Now I can fully focus on composing the music for my first compact disk. Strawberry and I just moved from Stone Mountain to Snapfinger Woods into a much larger apartment. I have room now to set up all my equipment and practice.

I like Snapfinger Woods even though I was burned out of here years ago. The area is very serene and remote, surrounded by acres of undeveloped land. They have ten different floor plans just for fifty units, and we have the largest one that they have to offer.

The apartment has four bedrooms, three bathrooms, two fireplaces, two porches, a living room, a dining room, a family room, and a kitchen. It is absolutely huge and expensive. It sits up on the third level, so it's high off the ground, overlooking the golf course.

Life is good and we are happy with each other; things couldn't be much better. Strawberry and I have been doing a lot of spontaneous traveling together over the past year. She loves the beach, so I have taken her to Florida several times. We also go to a lot of other places at a spur of the moment.

It's early one Friday evening. Strawberry and I are at her granny's house, and Dottie, her mother, wants a bottle of Canadian Mist from the liquor store. When I pull up in the parking lot, there is a crowd of guys hanging out in front of the store. Strawberry looks at me and says, "Go to another store because there is too many guys hanging out here."

I slowly reach under the seat and pull out my pistol. *Click, click.* I chamber a round and then pass her the .45. As I open the door to get out, I stop and look back at her and say, "If somebody bothers you and your life is threatened, point it at him and squeeze the trigger." She makes no comment, but she picks up the pistol and smiles.

I return to the car and ask her, "Did you have any trouble, baby?" She just smiles at me, and slowly she replies, "No, I didn't have any problems." I pull the magazine out of the pistol and point it at the floor between my legs to do a safety check. *Bang!* Oh shit, the gun fired and everyone standing in front of the store scatters like a flock of birds.

Damn, I didn't expect it to fire. I forgot that I chambered a round before I entered the store. I almost shot my own foot off; the bullet only missed me by a couple of inches. Strawberry is pissed off at me and holding her ears. I'm pretty sure that her ears are ringing because mine are too.

After we get back to her granny's house with the liquor, I go back outside to the car to take a good look at the bullet hole. Wow, from underneath the car, the bullet missed the brake lines by only three inches. I'm lucky that I still have my foot and the car is not damaged.

The next day, Strawberry and I go back to Kirkwood to take her mom grocery shopping. After she finished shopping, I decided to go a couple of blocks down the street to visit my cousins Esther and Clint. I usually stop by there from time to time just to sit around and talk with them.

I get to Esther's house, and most of her family is gathered here. Clint, Ricky, Regina, Bud, Shirley, and her kids are here. Shirley has the cutest little twin boys that you will ever see. Their father is the same guy that recruited me into the army. They are only about five years old, and they look exactly alike.

As some of us sit outside on the steps to the front door, we can hear the sound of the ice-cream truck coming toward us. "Hello, hello." And then the music plays. "Hello, hello." And then the music plays. Over and over and over, until the kids get all excited and start screaming for ice cream.

By the time the ice-cream truck stopped in front of the house, one of the twins starts running toward it. Everybody screams for him to stop because of an oncoming car speeding down the street carelessly. Within a blink of an eye, the unthinkable happens.

Boom! The car hits him and literally drags him underneath it for a hundred feet or more. Oh shit, everybody is running to the car, screaming and crying in disbelief. Unbelievably, he is still alive and calling for his brother with his last breath. I can hear him calling, "Bo, Bo, Bo, Bo," even though his little body is all mangled underneath the car. Then he passes away.

There is a trail of blood from the front of the house all the way to the stopped car, and it is a heartbreaking sight. Everyone is hysterical and blown away from what just happened. The driver of the car happens to be a fourteen-year-old girl trying to learn how to drive.

I know that there is a god, and I truly believe in him. Then I ask myself a question, why would God allow something like this to happen to such a sweet little kid? This is such a horrendous scene, and my little cousin is only five years old. I really can't understand why an innocent life is gone, just like that.

A few months pass, and my brothers, Donald and Rob, convince me to play another nightclub gig with them again. The gig is booked for Friday and Saturday night, at my old stomping grounds on Campbellton Road. I agree to play with them, knowing very well that there is no future in it. So I must admit that I do miss playing music with my brothers.

Strawberry decides to come along with me for the first show on Friday night. It's a good show because my brothers and I haven't been on the stage together for months. We are really feeling one another musically tonight and having a lot of fun.

Strawberry is sitting at the table with both of my brothers' wives, Shedra and Valerie. They seem to be enjoying themselves as well, drinking cocktails and tripping on us. I usually stay backstage between shows and let the rest of the band do the mingling. Tonight I can't do that because Strawberry is here, so after we play a forty-five-minute set, I sit at the table with my baby.

The next day, guess who calls me up. Yeah, you guessed it right, Red. She heard about the gig tonight and wants me to pick her up and take her with me to see us perform. Oh shit, I must be crazy because I told her that I would pick her up at ten o'clock. Strawberry told me earlier that she wasn't going tonight, so just maybe I can pull this off after all.

Red and I arrive at the club, and everybody is surprised to see her. She is looking absolutely fabulous, and there is no question about that. Last night it was Strawberry, but tonight she is sitting at the table with my brothers' wives. Shedra and Valerie may be a little reluctant to keep company with her, but then again they have a history together, so they enjoy themselves.

I am in the middle of singing Keith Sweat's song "How Deep Is Your Love." I have the crowd and especially the ladies all worked up into the song, and then, *bam!* Strawberry walks in the door. Oh shit. She is with her sister, and they immediately see Red and my brothers' wives sitting together, enjoying the show. She is just standing there, eyeballing me with the meanest look that I have ever seen from her.

I'm doing my best to maintain my composure and finish singing the song. After I do finish the song, Strawberry walks out the door and doesn't say a word to anyone. We still have one more song that we have to perform before the entire show is over. As soon as we play the last note, I'm going to check on her because I know that she wants to kill me right about now.

Red is just sitting at the table, smiling and enjoying the drama that she and I have caused. The bouncer of the club walks up to me as I'm leaving the stage and says, "Sergio, I think that you should go outside and check your BMW." Oh shit, Strawberry is standing in front of my car with a freaking six-foot-long steel pipe. I guess I'm too late because she has already busted out my windshield, and her sister is desperately trying to calm her down.

I look at her, then I look at the car. I look at her, then again the car. Slowly I turn to her and ask her, "Have you lost your freaking mind?" Now I'm pissed off. Even though I'm wrong for bringing Red to the show, I really think she went too far with this situation. Now I'm approaching her with anger and fire in my eyes, and everybody stops me before I get to her.

My brother Donald says, "Hey, man, just let it go because you can buy another windshield tomorrow if you want to." The biggest reason that I'm pissed off is because I have to drive with no windshield, and it is very cold right now. Actually it is starting to snow, and that is only going to make matters worse for my drive home. Not to mention that I have no idea as to what is in store for me once I get there.

Before I go home, I have to take Red home first. When I get into her parking lot, she looks at me and says, "Maybe you should come on in and let me warm you up before you go home, Sergio."

"Sure, why not?" I reply. After all the shit that I've been through tonight, I can use a little warming up.

I finally make it home, and Strawberry is sitting up, waiting for me. Before I can close the door behind me, she is already going off on me. "Sergio, I am sick and tired of your bullshit," she says. "If you want to be with Red, then you should go and be with her. When you do go to see her, you won't be a pretty boy anymore because I cut up all your shit."

"All of your fine suits and shoes have been cut to threads with a razor," she says. "If you want to jump on me and beat me up, then go right ahead and do it."

"Girl, you must be out of your mind. I am not going to lay a hand on you. As for the clothes and my car goes, I guess I deserved it and I understand your anger." She fell right into that one and immediately grabs me and squeezes me with a hug. She expected me to feed into her fight, but I remained cool and calm until she fell asleep.

Strawberry and I decided to stay together, but the last few months with her have been very difficult. She has no trust in me still. I thought by now I would've built at least a small amount of it back up. We rarely make love, and the relationship is scarred all because of my stupid decision.

I have started hanging out in the streets now, being that Strawberry is not showing me any love at home. The people that I hang out with are selling either powder cocaine or crack cocaine, and we go to a lot of stripper clubs to exploit the girls. After months of being around the drugs, I end up doing exactly what I said that I would never do. I just took my first hit of crack cocaine. Oh shit.

Damn, immediately after I exhale the smoke, I'm in a freaking zone. I have never felt anything like this before, and I'm scared because I feel too high, too fast. My heart is beating so fast that it feels like it is going to jump out of my chest. I'm so paranoid that I can't move, and when I try to speak, my mouth is going through the motions, but there is no sound coming out.

What the hell, everybody around me is looking crazy like they are beyond high, and I can immediately feel the presence of evil spirits enter the room. We're all just sitting here staring at the freaking walls and at one another like zombies. Nobody is saying a word. I am so ashamed of myself right now that I absolutely will not leave out the door and look this way.

After twenty minutes pass, my body, my mind, and my soul are craving for another hit of crack. I am so dead again. Every time that I inhale the smoke, it feels like I'm literally putting demons in my body. The strange thing about it is that I know that this is terrible, yet I still sit here and continue to smoke. I end up staying there all night and spending every dollar that I had in my pocket.

That night turned out to be the beginning of a serious addiction, because I have progressed rapidly with my crack-smoking ventures. Strawberry has been dealing with me patiently for over a year now, and today she finally asked me to leave. I was never there because I didn't ever want them to see me while I was high on crack. When I did finally show up, shit, I was broke.

I am not angry with Strawberry in any way, because she is a good woman. She stood by my side regardless of all the things that I put her through. I have not been there for her lately because the crack cocaine addiction has consumed me, and I can admit that.

This addiction is after my very soul, and Satan is sucking me in like a vacuum cleaner. I am literally dancing with the devil every time that I smoke crack because it can kill me. The only way that I'm going to be able to overcome this is through Jesus Christ, my Lord and Savior.

Mango

After being a lost soul out there in the streets for a year or so, I finally wake up one day and remember who I am. I am God's child and I belong to him. He has given me several skills and gifts to succeed in life, and Satan has been trying his best to destroy and kill me.

I have a good job again working for a Chevrolet dealership that is located only five minutes away from my new apartment. When I get off work and close the door behind me, it feels like I've been born again. I live alone in a huge three-bedroom apartment in Clarkston, and I'm at peace with myself.

I am now on my way back to work from having a quiet lunch at the crib. As I sit in front of the red light, waiting for the light to change, a black truck pulls up next to me. I look over, and damn, who is that? I see quite possibly the most beautiful girl in the world. The light changes to green, and she gives me this seductive smile as we make eye contact with each other.

When we pull up to the next red light, she has a ball of paper in her hand and tosses it in the car at me. "Nice convertible," she says. "My name is Mango, and my telephone number is on that ball of paper. Maybe you can give me a call later." I look at her and wink and say, "I'll see if I can make that happen for you."

Less than two hours later, I call her up, and she invites me out for the night. When I arrive at her house and get inside, I really check her out from head to toe. Her skin has the rich color and tone of silky caramel. Her hair is wavy, shiny, and as black as a raven, draped over her shoulders.

Her teeth are whiter than the ivory on a grand piano, and her lips are big and full of honey. Her eyes are like two body-armor-piercing bullets, able to penetrate any obstacle before it. She is meticulously dressed to kill, and those that do avoid death will still be wounded.

Mango is a step up from beautiful, because all my previous girlfriends were beautiful. This girl is absolutely stunning; she will make any guy and some women, as for that matter, do a double take to get a second look at her. If I were to guess her measurements, I would say that she is thirty-eight, twenty-four, thirty-eight. Damn, she is so fine.

As I admire her stunning beauty, my spirit tells me that there is something very different about Mango. I can't put my finger on it just yet, but I'm sure that it will reveal itself within time. After talking over a cocktail or two, we decide to go out and have dinner at a romantic little jazz spot in Midtown.

She's feeling me already, and I'm mutually feeling her as well. We decide to go back to my place instead of hers after dinner so that we can get better acquainted. She kisses me in one room, and then she quickly moves to another room. We play the cat-and-mouse game all over the apartment until she finally submits herself.

Mango is from St. Paul, Minnesota, and she says that she has only been living in Atlanta for three years. Her ex left her and her three boys in the house about four months ago. She has two sons, ages twelve and thirteen, that are back in Minnesota right now. Her youngest son, aged five, is with his father, the same guy that left her in the house.

After dating for about a month, she asks me if she can move in with me for a little while. She says that her house is in foreclosure and that she only needed to stay with me for a month. I have plenty of room, and I must admit that we have been enjoying each other for a month, so I look at her and say, "Sure, why not?"

No more than a week later, she learns about my goals and ambitions in the music industry. She is very optimistic and supportive, so immediately she starts working on all the paperwork needed for my three companies. I am trying to establish a record label, a production company, and a publishing company.

Mango is going to help me finance the project, so it seems like my dream to make an original recording is about to come to pass. What I tried to accomplish with my brothers for nine years is about to be done within three months. She is just as excited about the project as I am, and that makes me happy, very happy.

The thirty days pass and Mango isn't thinking about moving. She tells me that she is in love with me and that she would much rather stay here with me. I'm not in love with her yet, but I do care a lot about her, so I agree to let her stay. Who knows where this might go; I'll just have to play this one out and see.

A couple of days later when I arrive home from work, this girl has thrown out all my groceries and replaced it with all healthy shit. Everything in the kitchen is organic or all natural, and there are supplements and vitamins everywhere. "What the hell is this, and why did you throw out all of my shit?" I ask.

She says, "Sergio, that stuff wasn't good for you. From now on I'll be cooking you some healthy meals." The next day I get another surprise; one side of my smoking-room wall is covered with books from the floor to my waist. Almost all the books are about black magic, voodoo, mind manipulation, astrology, and all kinds of weird shit like that.

She has a library of audiotapes from several different motivational speakers. My spirit told me from the very beginning that this girl was going to be quite different from what I was accustomed to. Mango also likes to take extremely long walks. She and I walked completely around Stone Mountain one day, and I thought that I was going to die from trying to keep up with her.

She never tells me no when I want sex; as a matter of fact, I have to tell her no. She constantly comes at me sexually several times a day, as if she's trying to drain everything that I have within me. Sometimes I have to tell her that I have a headache, or that I'm tired, or sick, any lie that I can think of at that moment. Having sex with her every day burns me out. It is no longer pleasurable for me; it's like a freaking job.

Today she's taking me back to the tattoo parlor to get my first tattoo. It's an eagle flying across my chest, and the wingspan spreads from my collarbone to my heart. After leaving the tattoo parlor, she takes me to a barber to get my head shaved. Mango is on top of everything about this project, even down to the way I look.

She has booked a photo session for me within a couple of days, and we both think that the bald head would be better for my image. Mango takes the time to go over every little detail concerning this project, and I like her attentiveness.

Strawberry has been calling me periodically just to keep in touch with me. Before Mango moved in, she visited me here once or twice. Now she's wondering why I won't allow her to come over anymore. I'm sure that sooner or later, she's going to do a drive-by just to see what's going on.

When I moved in to this apartment, I had to leave my pit bull with a friend of mine that has a house. She's here with me in the apartment today because she just gave birth two days ago. She has seven puppies, and two of them are twins, because we watched as the both of them came out at the same time.

Mango and I decide that we will keep the twins and sell the rest of them once they are weaned. I decided to name the female Nikki, but Margo picked a name for the boy that I think is crazy; she wants to name him Lucifer. I look at her and ask, "Are you freaking serious? Do you really expect me to walk around calling out that name?"

"Absolutely," she says, and then she walks into the bedroom and closes the door. Five minutes later, she comes back out of the room butt naked, with her hair wrapped up in linen like she is from somewhere in Africa. I sit back and watch without saying a word to see what the hell she is going to do next.

This girl moves the coffee table from the middle of the floor and proceeds to the kitchen. When she returns from the kitchen, she has a five-pound bag of flour in her hands. She opens up the bag of flour, and then she draws a huge six-point star in the middle of the freaking floor. I'm still silent at this point and wondering, what now?

She picks up the little puppy that she wants to name Lucifer and says, "Look at his eyes, Sergio. They are closed just like all the rest of the puppies. Tomorrow, Lucifer's eyes will be open, and you will call him by his name."

"Yeah right," I reply. "I wouldn't hold my breath on that one if I were you."

She stands in the middle of the star and then falls to her knees with the puppy held up overhead by both hands. All of a sudden, she starts praying over the puppy, but she's speaking a language that I'm not familiar with. It's almost as if she were speaking in tongues, but why would somebody do that about a dog?

She gets off the floor and stands before me naked as if she is putting herself on display. After gazing into my eyes for a minute that seemed like an eternity, she says, "Sergio, you are a warlock and you don't even realize it. I can see a lot of spiritual power harnessed right inside of you, but you don't know how to release it."

I reply by saying, "No, I'm afraid you got that wrong, because I don't want any affiliation with Satan." I walk away from her and go into the bedroom to get ready for bed. Shortly afterward, she joins me, and before you know it, we are engaged in passionate lovemaking.

As we lie next to each other afterward, all of a sudden the bed starts shaking as if someone were underneath it. I look around the room, and nothing else is moving; it's just the freaking bed shaking. We silently look at each other as the bed begins to elevate a foot off the floor. Mango then squeezes me tightly from fear as the bed shakes itself back down.

"Sergio, Sergio, did you feel that? There is something in this room with us, and it isn't natural. I told you that there is power inside of you," she says. "The freaking bed came up off of the floor. Now how do you explain that?"

"I can't explain that," I reply. "What the hell was that?"

Mango and I talk for the rest of the night about paranormal and spiritual issues. She seems to be the only person besides my grandmother that recognizes a gift in me. Actually we have conversations about things that I have never told anyone. Most people would assume that I have some type of mental problem, if I have a conversation with them about certain things.

A couple of weeks later, I finally walk out of the studio with a finished product. I played the song in the car all the way home, and it is a thrill for me to hear my own music for the first time. I am waiting for five thousand copies, and I plan on selling the most of them.

For the next two weeks I've been putting up signs all over town about my first single release. I usually start at about three o'clock in the morning, and while everyone else is asleep, I'm going from place to place putting signs on telephone poles with a staple gun. It's a lot of work, but I can't expect anyone else to do it for me.

Finally, after all the preparations and obstacles, I'm looking at a wall full of boxes that are loaded with my compact disks. I take a knife and cut the tape off the first box and pull out a disk for inspection. Damn, it's exactly the way that I wanted it. Now comes the hard part; I have to sell these disks.

The first thing I have to do is hit all the record stores and set up a consignment agreement with them. After that, I guess that I'm going to have to hit the bricks and sell this shit in the streets. I'm going to need a one-liner that will be effective for all ages and races. It doesn't matter if they listen to this type of music or not. I still have to sell these disks.

I got it. I know exactly what I will say to everyone that I come in contact with. "Excuse me, my name is Sergio and I'm a local artist from here in this community. I have a small record label that I am trying to get off of the ground, and I was wondering if I could get your support by purchasing one of my disks." Hell yeah, I think that will work.

Before long, I'm walking in the door every night with a pocket full of money and an empty bag of disks. Mango is enjoying observing my hustle every night, but now she is getting concerned about my safety. Tonight as I was walking out of the door, she stops me and gives me a kiss. While she is kissing me, she is also slipping a pistol under my belt.

She looks up at me with her beautiful big eyes and says, "That's just in case one of them niggas do something stupid and try to take your money." Then she says, "I'm pregnant, Sergio, and I don't want anything to happen to you out there." I can't believe my ears. Did this girl just tell me that she is pregnant, or am I tripping? I drop the bag of disks on the floor and embrace her as tears of joy drop from her eyes.

There is no way that I'm going out tonight and sell disks. I'd rather be home and pamper Mango. Here I go again with this baby stuff, and when I get all excited about it, something bad happens. Well, once again I hope that it's a girl so that I can spoil her rotten.

The next day I get a phone call from Strawberry at work, and she's getting jealous about Mango being there. She thinks that Mango has some type of a voodoo spell on me and that I will be hurt by her. She seems to be quite convinced that Mango is using negative forces to keep me with her. I'm literally blown away because Strawberry knows nothing about the books in my crib that's based on that exact subject matter.

When I get home from work, Mango is sitting on the sofa, looking disturbed by something. So I ask her, "Hey, baby, are you feeling all right, or is something wrong with you?"

"You damn right something is wrong with me, Sergio," she says. "Before I talk to you about it, I would like to show you something," she says.

She pulls out a book and says that her dad wrote it and that the book was about his life as a gangster in the Midwest and up north. He served twelve years in prison for a murder charge and became an evangelist once he was released. She shows me pictures of herself in the book with her dad as a child.

Then she looks me in the eyes and says, "My dad was a part of the Mafia, and before he died, they promised him that they would look after me. So no matter where I go or who I choose as my man, they always check things out. With that being said, Sergio, now I will tell you what is bothering me."

"Today you talked to your ex-girlfriend Strawberry on the phone at work. I know exactly what time she called you. I also know her home address, job address, driver's license number, social security number, birthday, height, and weight."

"Get out of here," I say to her in a sarcastic, laughing manner.

"There is nothing that you can do out there in the streets, Sergio, that won't be revealed to me," she says. "Who are you, the freaking police?" I ask. "Do you think that you can just come in my life and push me around like a little bitch? No, I don't think so," I reply.

Now she has really pissed me off, and I'm wondering, was that a freaking threat? We spend most of the evening barely saying anything to each other and looking the other way. After we get in bed and fall asleep, the telephone starts ringing. I look at the clock, and it is two o'clock in the morning, so I'm a little annoyed that someone would be calling me this late.

I look over at Mango and say, "Whoever is on the phone must have an emergency to call this late, so this better be good." I answer the phone, and someone is on the other end talking to me through a voice-altering device; they sound like freaking RoboCop. I sit up in the bed and listen as they tell me about places that I have been and people that I have seen.

Whoever is on the other end of the phone knows a lot of personal shit about me. The amount of information he has is prodigious, and I'm absolutely speechless. After telling me all the things that he knows about me, he then proceeds to the threats. Not to harm me, but to harm someone that I am close to.

After I hang up the phone, I look over at Mango, and she is just lying there under the covers as if nothing is going on. I tap her on the shoulder and ask, "Who in the hell was that, and why did you give them my personal information?" She turns her head toward me and say, "Sergio, I just told you earlier about them folks, so you better watch yourself."

Now I feel like I have to watch my back everywhere I go, and it's an uneasy feeling. Two weeks later, Strawberry calls me again at work, and she says that her mother is in the hospital and that she wants to see me. On my way home from work, I stop by my mom's place to visit with her for a moment. While I'm there, I decide to call Strawberry and let her know that I will be at the hospital later.

I get home, and Mango is busy reading one of her black-magic books, so I take a shower and change clothes. I let her know that I'm leaving out for a couple of hours and hit the door. I drive from home to a train station, I take the train to another station, I catch a cab from the train station to the hospital, all in an effort to elude being followed.

Strawberry's mom is very sick, but when she sees me, her eyes light up with joy. She loves me like a son, and I love her too, so there was no way that I was not going to go there and be by her side in time of need. Strawberry is looking at the way her mother and I interact with each other, and she is emotionally touched. I can see the tears building up in her eyes, and they are just about to fall down her face.

After my brief visit with Strawberry and her mom, I head back to the crib. When I walk in the door, Mango is sitting on the sofa with a serious attitude. I can see it all over her face. She immediately starts telling me every move that I made, from the phone call at work to the phone call at my mom's house.

She then proceeds to tell me about the elusive route that I took just to get to the hospital. She knows who I went to see; she also knows that Strawberry was there. This girl knows every freaking thing. Before she can finish saying all that she has to say, the telephone rings.

Oh shit, it's freaking RoboCop again, and he tells me all the same shit that Mango just said. He threatened to hurt Strawberry's little grandbaby, who is only a couple of months old. He even knows that the baby has green eyes; now how in the hell could he know that without being up close enough to see them for himself?

This shit is getting deep, and now I'm starting to get seriously concerned about the people around me. As I'm working the next day inside the shop, I feel a sense of being watched by someone. I have a car raised on the lift, and I am standing underneath it, inspecting for leaks.

Oh shit, the freaking devil just walked inside the shop, and he is headed straight toward me. I'm the only person who is inside the shop that can see it. It is freaking huge; it must be ten feet tall and five hundred pounds or more.

It has slobber dripping from the sides of his mouth, and his eyes are the eyes of death. He is not a man; he is a creature, and a terrifying one at that. His body blends in with everything that is around him, just like the movie Predator. He's coming for me, and I'm not standing here to see what happens next.

I drop my tools and take off running to my vehicle in the parking lot. I never look back to see how close the devil is; I just run like hell. I finally make it to my car and drive straight to a church. As I sit there in the parking lot with the engine still running, I can't believe what just happened.

I got the freaking Mafia investigating my every move and the damn devil coming at me while I work. Somebody please tell me, what is going on? Sure, I have seen images of the devil many of times in my dreams while I was asleep. Now he's coming at me in broad daylight, with me wide awake, and freaking people around.

Tomorrow I have to explain to my employer why I ran out of the shop and just left the customer's car up in the air. I know that it looked strange for me to just drop what I was doing and take off running, but if they saw what I did, they would have ran too.

For the next couple of weeks, I cut off all contact with Strawberry. I even stopped my family and friends from stopping by because Mango says that they all want to have sex with her. She has managed to pull off one of the oldest tricks in the book on me.

Divide and conquer, she has separated me from everyone through fear and insecurity. The only voices that I hear now are hers and freaking RoboCop's. No one visits me, and I don't call anyone. Strawberry swears that Mango has voodoo on me. She has been saying that from the very beginning.

Mango's stomach is getting to be huge, and I think that she may have twins. I suggest that she have an ultrasound done in order to determine the sex of the baby, but I don't mention to her that I expect her to be carrying twins.

The following day she does just as I asked her to and goes to the doctor. The doctor finally comes out with the results and says, "Congratulations, it's a girl, and she has a sister with her. They are twins."

"Oh shit," Mango says, "are you serious, Doc?"

"Yes, ma'am, I am absolutely serious. You have a set of healthy twin girls."

I knew it already; not only was she getting too big too fast, but it was revealed to me through spirit. When we arrived back home, someone had spread salt all the way up the stairs to my front door. It took us both a minute to figure out who would do such a thing, and it is Strawberry. She is very adamant concerning Mango being involved with witchcraft.

RoboCop has been calling me lately and threatening me about marrying Mango. He says that if I don't marry her, he is going to have someone killed in my family. This has gotten to the point where I'm truly in fear of something happening. So I finally agree to marry her.

Mango is in an awful hurry to marry me because she wants to go to the courthouse as soon as possible. I'm still trying to figure out her motive because I don't believe that she loves me that much. Two days later, I leave my job for lunch and meet her at the courthouse to get it over with. Immediately afterward, I return to work, as if nothing happened.

Damn, I'm married now and I'm supposed to be happy, but that is not the case. I try to be on my best behavior for the sake of the marriage and the twins on the way, but deep down in my heart, I know that this isn't right. Mango is too manipulative, and she wants to control my every move.

A week passes by and I haven't heard from RoboCop with any threats, so maybe I'm doing all right now. I walk in the door from work, and there is something different about the way Mango looks. I walk by her and go into the bedroom to get a change of clothes, when it hits me.

Damn, I run back into the living room to get another look at her, and her freaking stomach is gone. It's as flat as it can be, and she can't look at me in the eyes. "What the hell happened to your stomach?" I ask. "Did you abort my babies?" She looks at me with tears in her eyes and says, "Yes, Sergio, I aborted the babies."

"Who in their right freaking mind would kill five-month-old twin girls?" I ask. "Furthermore, what kind of doctor would do such a thing this late? Five freaking months, are you kidding me?" I ask. "Are you a freaking monster? What in the hell is wrong with you, Mango?"

I'm crushed and devastated. I can't believe that she did such a thing. Who does that? Nobody in their right mind would kill two little babies that are five months old. This bitch is evil, and I must get away from her as soon as possible. Damn, I have married the devil's daughter, and she is going to try to destroy me.

I go for weeks without touching her, and now she is starting to get frustrated with me. As I awaken this morning, my spirit is leading me to go to church, but I have no church home, so I have to choose one at random. I chose to go to World Changers International and listen to Dr. Creflo Dollar, and it was a good choice because as soon as I entered the door, I felt the presence of the Lord.

Sitting here listening to Mr. Dollar, I have received the Holy Ghost in my spirit several times. He is a great teacher, and all the things that I was taught as a youngster and have been away from are coming back to me. When he asked if there is anyone that wanted to dedicate their life to Jesus, I jumped at the opportunity. Even though I was saved as a child, I want to rededicate my life to Jesus.

As soon as I arose from my knees in prayer, I felt the power of the Lord restored within me. I am born again, and my spirit has been renewed. I am no longer going to live in fear because ultimately God is in control, not Mango or RoboCop. So the next time that I'm confronted with their threats, they are going to be surprised by my response.

When I get back home, I have a smile on my face, my head is held high, and my spirit has been lifted. It is obviously noticeable because Mango asks, "Was church that good, Sergio?"

"Yes, you should have been there," I reply in a sarcastic sort of way. She just rolls her eyes at me and toots up her nose. I look back at her and smile because she has no idea that Jesus is with me now.

Months go by and I have been a different person, reading the Word and going to church. She doesn't know what to make of me now, and she knows that our relationship is fugacious. I've even come up with a plan to get away from her. I'm going to leave her and go back to Florida. Once I get there, I will start all over again as a free man.

Two weeks later, it's a done deal. I'm in Florida and free from Mango. I left her with everything in the crib, except for my clothes. She knows that I am here, and she also knows how to get here because I brought her here several times. I don't think that she will leave the city to follow me here, so I'm good for now.

I have been in Florida for three months, and I have found a good job as manager for an auto repair shop. My dad and stepmother are renting me one of their houses, and I'm at peace now. The only problem that I have is Mango calling me every day, talking about how much she loves and misses me.

A month later she arrives in Florida with a freaking moving truck full of all our shit from Atlanta. She says, "Sergio, you are my husband, and I am not going to let you go just like that without a fight, so here I am." Damn, she is my wife, so what's a brother supposed to do in a situation like this? She has packed up all this shit and found me, and I don't have the heart to turn my back on her at this point.

We spend the next couple of days rearranging the house to accommodate the both of us. After everything is set up, we have a nice dinner together and discuss our future plans with each other. I have a very forgiving nature, so I put everything that she done to me in the past behind me and close that chapter.

Six months pass and we have been getting along just fine. My oldest brother, Ronald, has been living in Florida ever since he retired from the military, and he's going to Atlanta for the weekend to see our mom. He asked me to ride with him, and I agreed because I would love to see my mom and family.

Mango is upset about me going to Atlanta. She thinks that I'm going there just to see Strawberry, and she promises me that I will not make it there. I don't want to fuss and fight about it, so I came up with a plan. Every day for lunch this week, I will go home for lunch and slip out an outfit and take it to my brother's house.

When Friday comes, I won't have to leave out with a suitcase; all I will have to do is get in the car and go. My brother is going to be driving his car, so everything will already be packed up when he pulls into the driveway. This way, I can leave quietly without having an argument with her and without having a big scene created.

Friday comes quickly, and I'm leaving my job, headed home to change clothes before my brother arrives. I pull up in the driveway and get out of the car, but before I can get my house key in the door, I'm ambushed by six police officers. "Get on the ground! Get on the ground! Get your ass on the ground now!" they scream.

Four officers swooped in on me from the front, and two more came from the backyard. "What is going on?" I ask. "What in the hell is all this about?"

"Are you Sergio?" he asks. "Yes, I am," I reply, "so will you please tell me what the hell is going on?"

"Sir, you are under arrest for domestic violence and sexual assault."

"What in the hell is sexual assault?" I ask. "Sir, it is rape?" He replies, "Rape."

"Are you freaking kidding me?" I ask. "And on whom was this rape allegedly committed?"

"Your wife," he replies. "She says that you beat her up pretty bad twice and that you also raped her twice."

"My wife, you have to be freaking kidding me," I reply, "because I have to tell her that I have a headache."

As they put me in the backseat of the car, handcuffed like a common criminal, I have all kinds of thoughts running through my head. I look down the street, and Mango is pulling out of the driveway of one of my neighbors' house. She has been sitting there the whole time, watching this unfold. She slowly drives by the police car that I'm sitting in and says, "Nigga, I told you that you wasn't going to Atlanta to see your bitch."

Damn, that hit me right in the heart, so now I'm trying to figure out a way to get out of jail. I'm thinking, *Hey, I have a thousand dollars in my pocket, so maybe I can bond out.* When they book me into the jail, I found out that all four charges are felonies that carry a twenty-five-thousand-dollar bond on each. My bond is a hundred thousand dollars, and it looks like I'm not going anywhere anytime soon.

I tell my dad not to bond me out, instead to take the ten thousand dollars and get me a lawyer because I am innocent. I have never laid hands on Mango in any type of way, and surely I didn't rape her; hell, her sexual appetite is much greater than mine.

They strip-searched me and sprayed me with chemicals before showering and changing me into their clothes. I am so depressed and lost right now. I have never been locked up and treated this way before, so I'm really devastated. They put me in a cell with a guy that is locked up for possession of crack cocaine.

After two days they shackle me up like a slave with chains around my ankles and waist. The handcuffs are attached to the chain around my waist, so I look like a freaking dangerous person. I'm going to my first arraignment in front of a judge, and this is the way they transport inmates.

As I shuffle my feet across the floor like a slave bound in chains to stand in front of the judge, Mango is sitting across the room, crying as if she were terrified by the sight of me. My attorney looks at me and says, "Don't worry about her little play acting because I'm going to eat her alive in court. She actually used a false name when she married you, so technically she is not your wife."

My bond remains at one hundred thousand dollars, and I'm escorted back to the jail. The next day the nurse comes by to check me for tuberculosis; they gave me a shot two days prior. If a bump comes up on your arm that is bigger than a dime, you are most likely positive, and my bump is borderline.

They want to retest me again, but I'm already pissed off about being here, so I become defiant. "Hell no, you are not sticking me again," I tell the nurse. She is insisting that I do a retest, and I'm telling her to go to hell because I don't have any freaking tuberculosis. Finally, she gives up on getting me to retest and leaves.

Ten minutes later, two officers come to my cell. They demand me to pack up my things because they are taking me away from the general public. I will now be treated like a tuberculosis patient. They put me in an isolated cell with a loud-ass fan in the ceiling to suck out my bad air.

They only allow me to come out of the cell for fifteen minutes a day, just to take a shower. Whenever I come out of the cell, I have to wear a freaking mask as if I'm poison or something. After weeks of people calling me the tuberculosis man and pointing fingers at me, I finally break down and cry my heart out. I feel like the Lord has forsaken me; why is he allowing these people to treat me this way?

I fall down to my knees and bury my face in the floor and start praying. My grandmother's spirit enters the cell, and she's sitting in the corner, singing "Amazing Grace." The Holy Ghost takes over my body, and I am now praying in tongues with the correctional officers watching me in amazement.

Two days later, to my surprise, they call me to be released. I was facing twenty years on these charges, and the Lord has delivered me from the hands of the devil. "Thank you, Jesus. Thank you, Lord," I keep saying to myself over and over.

My attorney went to the state prosecutor and convinced her to drop the sexual assault charges for lack of evidence. Mango did not have a scratch on her anywhere whatsoever; furthermore, she didn't seek any medical attention. They never did a rape kit on her because it never happened.

Up until these false accusations were brought forth, I had no criminal history. The prosecutor also dropped the felony domestic violence charges down to misdemeanor battery. My bond went from one hundred thousand to four thousand, so I bonded out with four hundred dollars. Who says that God isn't still performing miracles? He is an awesome god.

Three days after my release, the Lord blesses me with a white Mercedes Benz that I had been looking at before my arrest. Also, Strawberry is here from Atlanta to see me. This girl has always had my back no matter what, and I will always love her for that.

I'm a little uncomfortable being in Florida now as long as Mango is here. All she has to do is call the police again and say that I'm harassing her, and then I'll be right back in jail. I am not going to give her that opportunity, so I'm going back to Atlanta with Strawberry. I know that as soon as I cross over the state line and see the sign that says "Welcome to Georgia," I'll feel like I'm born again.

Peaches

While driving up the interstate, my mind is replaying the events of the police ordering me to get on the ground, with their weapons drawn out on me. I have never felt so violated as I felt when they made me undress and sprayed freaking chemicals in my private area. The entire ordeal was such a humiliating experience, and I never want to go through that again.

Today, I am free and riding up the road in a white Mercedes Benz, with the windows down, enjoying the fresh air. There is an old saying that says "What a difference a day makes." They should change that to "What a difference my god makes." I feel like a mountain has been removed from on top of me. I was facing twenty years. Damn, there's my favorite sign in front of me, "Welcome to Georgia."

Strawberry has invited me to stay with her and her dad, so I go straight there and set up camp. She has me sleeping in the room with her even though there is a spare room available. So I'm assuming that this is going to be all good. Her dad is happy to have me here; he has always been quite fond of me and has treated me like a son.

It only takes me a week and I have a job in Riverdale. The house is on Bouldercrest Road, so my commute back and forth is not too bad considering the Atlanta traffic. When I get to the house, Strawberry is out most of the time. I haven't said anything to her about it yet, but I know something is going on.

It doesn't take long before the truth came to light. Something is going on; she's seeing another man. So I ask her, "Why in the hell would you bring me to your dad's house and sleep in your bed if you had no intentions on being with me?" She's speechless as she packs up her clothes to move out. Strawberry is leaving me in her room, at her dad's house; now isn't that some shit.

Later, her dad and I sit back like two real niggas and talk about the scenario over cocktails. He's a cool old dude and he really likes me; he said that I was welcome to stay there as long as I want. I can even bring other girls over if I want to; now how cool is that.

I'm still hurt because I didn't expect that from Strawberry. She has never denied me her love and attention, until now. As I think back on all the shit that I put her through, I guess I had it coming. I deserve exactly what she gave me, high expectations and a freaking heartbreak. So all I can do now is man up and move on.

Damn, this might not be so bad after all. I'm a good-looking brother, I have a job, and I'm riding hard. Give me a minute or two, and I'll be back in my own crib, on full attack mode. In the meantime, I'll just run these girls through Strawberry's dad's house as he suggested. Hell, all he wants to do is have a pretty girl in his presence.

It's on now; the ladies are hitting on me, and I'm hitting on them. I have enough telephone numbers to share with a friend, and I can't find enough time to spend with them all. The old man is like, "Damn, son, maybe you should slow down a little bit before you make a baby." I just look at him and smile and say, "No, sir, I am not trying to have any babies."

The next day I decide to visit my sister in the Dale. I haven't been in that neighborhood for a while, so maybe I can see a few other people while I'm there. When I walk in the door, my sister is getting her hair done by this cute, dark-skinned petite dime piece. She is blushing her ass off as my sister introduces us. She says, "Hi, Sergio, my name is Peaches, and it's a pleasure to meet you." I reply, "No, ma'am, the pleasure is all mine," as I slowly raise her hand to my lips and gently kiss it.

She immediately looks at my sister, smiling, and says, "Ooh shit, I'm going to have this nigga's baby." I hang around until she finishes my sister's hair so that I can give her a ride home and get better acquainted with her. She is very cute, and she carries herself as if she knows it. Surprisingly she has no kids, and she is the baby out of five siblings.

It doesn't take long for me to sweep her off her feet, and I genuinely do like her a lot. Lately we've been spending a lot of time together, and things are starting to get a little serious. The old man sees her coming out of my room constantly. Just the other day, he said, "Sergio, you are going to get that girl pregnant."

I like the old man and I really appreciate him allowing me to stay here for cheap rent, but the time has come for me to move on. I found a beautiful three-bedroom apartment in Buckhead, and today is my move-in day. The Lord works in mysterious ways, because I have been offered a new job that pays more money, located in the same area. So that means no more fighting traffic in order to get to work.

Damn, this is so cool. My apartment is only two blocks away from my job, and I come home for lunch every day. There is also a huge music store down the street where I spend a lot of my time. It has inspired me to record another project; this time it is going to consist of several different artists.

Weeks go by and I finally have my crib set up the way I want it. I'm really starting to like this prestigious area because I'm surrounded by people with money. Mostly everyone that I see living in this area is happy and enjoying life. So I'm going to suck up as much of this positive energy from here as I can. This is truly the lifestyle for me. I really don't belong in the hood.

Peaches rarely comes over here because she says that she doesn't want to be around all these white folks. Her mother has a beautiful home in Decatur that is located in a predominately black neighborhood. She's a mama's little girl still; she hasn't spent the night with me here once yet. Tonight she's coming over because she says that she has something to talk to me about, and I'm wondering what might that be.

I pick her up, and on the way to my crib, she is only talking about her customers. She does hair for a living, and she likes to tell me about their gossip. After having a nice, quiet dinner, we finally get close to each other and begin to cuddle. She looks up into my eyes and smiles and then says, "Sergio, we're going to have a baby. I am pregnant."

"Oh shit," I reply, "are you serious? Are you really pregnant?"

"Yes, baby," she says, "I'm pregnant and I am so happy." In my mind my immediate reaction is *Oh damn, here I go again with another pregnancy.* Reluctantly, deep down inside I'm a little paranoid that something might go wrong with this pregnancy, just as it did with Strawberry and Mango.

Months pass and Peaches is getting bigger and bigger; she seems to be doing just fine so far. She goes to the doctor frequently, and I am always right there by her side. I also attend all the parenting classes with her. This is her first child, so she is extremely excited about the whole ordeal.

She has three older sisters, and they are all married to ministers and have kids. Her mother is extremely religious, and every Sunday she cooks a huge dinner for the family. Her mother also belongs to a church different from that of her sons-in-law, and the minister of that church always comes over for dinner as well. So here I am, the bad boy, sitting at the table with four ministers having dinner.

It's all good though. I like the skin that I'm in. I always just remain myself because it makes no sense to put on, to be someone other than who I am. As a matter of fact, they like and respect me for that. I'm particularly fond of the eldest sister. She absolutely has the spirit of an angel from heaven. I must admit that Peaches's mother seemed to have instilled a lot of good values in all her daughters.

Months later, Peaches finally reaches the ninth month of her pregnancy, and she looks like she is going to pop wide open. She is so freaking big, and mean too. She snaps at me about every little thing; nothing seems to satisfy her now. I will be so glad when she delivers this baby and gets back to normal.

Three days later, I get the phone call that Peaches is on her way to deliver. Oh shit, the time has come for the baby to be born, so I rush to the hospital to be by her side. When I get there, she is almost but not quite ready yet. After I walk her around the halls of the hospital for thirty minutes, finally her water breaks.

As she lies on the delivery bed with her legs spread wide open, I stand at her feet, encouraging her to push. Damn, the head just popped out. What the, oh shit. This looks like something out of a science fiction movie. The baby is slowly coming out of her vagina. Seeing this gives me a whole new perspective on the female anatomy. Damn, the power of a woman is phenomenal.

It's a boy, and he is absolutely beautiful; I mean really. All parents think that their baby is cute, but this little baby boy is exceptionally beautiful. The doctor says, "Congratulations, you're now the parents of a healthy, beautiful baby boy." Then he looks at me and says, "Sergio, I would like to give you the honor of cutting the cord." After I cut the cord, I close my eyes and thank the Lord for a healthy baby and proceed outside to smoke a big, fat cigar.

The next day I'm enjoying myself while shopping for the baby. I have bought the best of everything that he needs, a baby bed, stroller, high chair, walker, clothes, diapers, formula, bottles, toys, and all the other little items that he needs. Peaches is on cloud nine, and I have never seen her happier. Everyone is complimenting her on how beautiful the baby is, and she is just eating it up.

Two months later I surprise Peaches by getting on my knees and proposing to her. She says yes, and she is absolutely overwhelmed with joy as I put the ring on her finger. The ring is nothing less than gorgeous, and it should be, because I paid three thousand dollars for it. She then slowly looks up at me with tears in her eyes, and her voice begins to tremble as she says, "I love you so much, Sergio."

"I love you too, baby," I reply, as I gently place my lips to her forehead. The relationship between us has been very complaisant for the past year, so I'm willing to give marriage and being a family my best efforts. I have yet to see a cantankerous attitude from Peaches. She is always sweet and soft-spoken.

Months later I try to pick up my son and take him along with me to visit my family, but Peaches won't allow it. I understand that this is her first child and that she maybe a little overprotective, but hey, I am the father. Not only can I not pick him up to leave with me, but she has also never brought the baby over to my place to spend the night.

We've been engaged for months now, and she still doesn't spend any time at my place. I also feel that her family is influencing her to keep the baby at their place, as if nowhere else is good enough for him. I have a beautiful apartment in one of the most prestigious neighborhoods in the city, but she seems to have a problem with being here.

Since I've known Peaches's family, they have always had this little contumelious attitude about themselves. It's never really bothered me until now, being that my son is involved. It's a good thing to walk around with your head held high, but to walk around with your nose turned up at other people is a whole different issue.

Now that the baby is here, they make me feel like I'm not good enough to keep him on my own because I don't attend church as regularly as they do. I already failed with my first son, by not being there for him when he was young. I definitely don't want to repeat the same mistake; that's why I've been adamant about taking care of him and spending time with him.

Peaches doesn't know it yet, but tomorrow I have to pick up a BMW that I just bought. I'm going to surprise her and let her drive it. This way, whenever she needs to take my son somewhere, she won't have to wait for a ride. Hopefully, she will use the car to bring my son to visit me on a regular basis, since she won't move in with me.

Since I really haven't been seeing much of Peaches and the baby, I've been focusing on my music. I'm working with three different rap groups, and all of them are pretty tight. I produced and recorded two songs for each group and made a compilation disk. Any day now I should be getting five thousand copies to sell, and it is perfect timing because Freaknic, the big annual college event, is going down next week.

One of the groups is called the Project Babies, and I'm a little more impartial to them because they are the youngest yet the tightest. Then there's the group SDG, whom I'm quite fond of as well. Last but not least is Diamond D, who is my sister's son. All of them did a great job performing on my tracks, so I'm eagerly awaiting the shipment of my disks.

A week later, I pick up the shipment of disks, and the rappers are extremely excited to see a finished product. Each disk is individually silk wrapped, and the print layout on the inside jacket is as tight as the cover design. In the midst of all the excitement, one of the rappers has the audacity to ask me how long it is going to be before we make the video.

I slowly look at him, and then I look back at the boxes of disks stacked up on the wall and say, "As soon as you make me some of my freaking money back, fool." I said that to him because I know that he is not going to put any effort into selling these disks. He wants everything handed out to him on a silver platter.

It takes me a couple of weeks, but I managed to single-handedly get the disks into all the independent record stores in the city. I also was able to get them on the shelf of two nationally known record stores through a consignment program. Then I gave away approximately a thousand disks to college students that were from out of town, in an effort to spread the music outside Atlanta.

I was able to convince the most influential hip-hop radio host in the city to allow me to meet with him. As I enter the building and proceed to take the elevator to the radio station, guess who gets on the elevator with me. Oh shit, it's Master P, C-Murder, and Silkk the Shocker of No Limit Records. Damn, I'm freaking rubbing elbows with the big boys now, at least for the moment.

This is crazy because I had also talked with another radio host from a gospel station, and I had an appointment to see him today as well. I write and compose gospel music just as well as I do hip-hop, and today I had a choice of going to the gospel station or the hip-hop station. I guess you can say that my flesh won that battle, because here I am at the hip-hop station, sitting next to nationally known rappers.

This experience feels great right now, but deep down inside I know that I made the wrong decision. I should've gone to the gospel station like God told me to do, but no, I chose to do what I want to do. I think all the way back to when I was just a kid playing drums in church, I knew from then that the Lord wanted me to play for him. I just hope that I don't end up like Jonah, in the belly of the whale for not doing what I was told to do by God.

Three days later I'm back at work. It's been a very busy day, being that I am the only certified technician in the shop. As I work underneath a car, replacing an oil pan gasket, all of a sudden I hear something that sounds very familiar. Oh shit, it's my freaking song with Diamond D, and they're playing it on the radio. I drop the tools in my hand and stand there in disbelief as I listen to my song over the airways.

After the song goes off, the radio host gives me a shout-out, and it's all good. I look at myself with the oil and dirt all over my hands and say to myself, "One of these days, I won't have to do this anymore." After work, I go straight home to get cleaned up before heading to the hood. As I come out of the shower, I hear the radio station playing another song of mine; this time it's the Project Babies.

Wow, now I really feel a sense of accomplishment. That was just the confirmation that I needed to let me know that my music has merit. As I enter into the hood, the kids are calling my name out loud at every corner. I assume that they heard the songs on the radio, because they have never acted this way before. Furthermore, word travels fast in the hood, so most of them know about it anyway.

In the hood, things are all good. Everybody who assumes that they have talent is approaching me about producing music for them. I'm getting attention from people that normally wouldn't even speak to me. In my mind I'm thinking, *Slow down, people, I haven't made any money off of this shit yet.* Just because my music was played on the radio doesn't mean that I'm going to make millions; it simply doesn't work that way.

The Dale is very close to where Peaches and her mom live, so after I leave the hood, I go there to visit her and my son for the rest of the evening. The both of them are doing fine, and the baby is growing so fast. I really wish that we were all living under the same roof so that I can be a full-time dad. I don't like having to go to her mother's house as my only option to see my son.

The next day I surprise Peaches with a beautiful BMW for her to drive, equipped with a brand-new car seat for the baby. I wonder what her excuse is going to be now for not coming over to my crib. Furthermore, we are engaged to be married, so there should be no obstacle in the way of our relationship. I want her to be able to come to me whenever she wants to see me.

A month later my lease is up on the apartment, and she never did come by to spend one night with me here, what a waste. I found a newly renovated house in the Dale, and tomorrow I will be moving in to it. I decided to move back into the hood since Peaches was adamant about not living in a predominately white neighborhood.

After a couple of days, I have everything moved and set up just the way I want it. It's kind of nice being back in the hood because my mom and sister still live in this area. I can literally go by and see them every day if I choose to, being that they are only two blocks away from me. I'm also closer to the rappers that I produced, so it's easier for me to rehearse with them and have meetings when needed.

A couple of weeks pass and this girl hasn't stepped a foot in my crib yet. Wait a minute, something has got to be going on with this girl. How can she be only three miles away from me, ride around in my shit with a three-thousand-dollar ring on her finger, and not come to visit me? Who does that, and why won't she bring the baby over to spend time with me? Maybe I should call the *Maury* show and see if he says "Sergio, you are not the father."

I decide to pop up on her little ass instead and catch her off guard. The first thing that I notice is that she is not wearing the ring on her finger. "Where is the ring?" I ask. She says, "Sergio, I am so sorry, but I lost it and didn't know how to tell you."

"Are you freaking serious?" I ask. "Do you have any idea as to how that makes me feel? How in the hell can you lose a freaking ring that's fitted to your finger?"

I am so pissed off now; as a matter of fact, I'm hotter than a Saturday night special, on a Friday night. So I look into her eyes and say, "You know what, I am done with you, Peaches. Give me the freaking keys to my BMW, and I'll go ahead and kick bricks. I have done everything that I can to please you, and now I'm freaking done with you. I have no problem with taking care of my son, but as far as you and I are concerned, this shit is over, shorty, deuces."

Candy

The music is going as well as to be expected, and I have made most of my money back. I have been trying to get these groups to perform at different nightclubs so that they can get some exposure. They are so freaking hard-headed, and they think that they know everything already. They sit on their ass week after week without making any attempts to perform in clubs or sell the disks.

As soon as I get my money back, I am done with these guys, and I will definitely not reinvest into another project with them. I have gotten no assistance whatsoever with the real work that is involved in a project like this. I have to do all the footwork by myself while they sit back as if they are celebrities or something. Since they have heard themselves on the radio, they think that the work is done, but in reality the work has just begun.

Months pass and I have been spending a lot of my time alone. I don't care for the nightclub scene anymore unless I'm performing there, and I don't like to hang out with a bunch of guys because that only brings trouble. I am quite content with being alone, considering the relationships that I've been through.

An old friend of mine stopped by the house today and informed me that he gave my number to a lady that needs her car repaired. He said that she would be calling me any day now to set up an appropriate time for me to check it out. He also said that I just might be interested in her once I meet her, because she is very attractive.

Two hours later she calls, and she wants me to come over to her crib now and diagnose the problem with her car. When I get to her apartment complex, I call her to let her know that I am outside, in the parking lot. As soon as she comes out of her apartment and I take one look at her, damn, it's lust at first sight. It usually takes me some time before I really like someone, but I like this girl now.

She says, "Hi, Sergio, I'm Candy. Did you have any problems finding the place?"

"No, ma'am," I reply, "you gave me good directions, and I didn't have any problems at all getting here." As she passes me her car keys, I can feel my heart rate speed up from excitement or nervousness, or maybe a little of both. This girl is so tall, maybe six foot two or six foot three. She is actually standing over me by a couple of inches.

After I diagnosed and repaired her car, I invited her to come over to my place later this evening for a couple of cocktails. To my surprise she quickly accepted the invite, so I'm excited on my way back home to get everything in order. Candy has all the features of an Indian; her skin tone has a reddish tint to it, and her hair is extremely long, jet-black, and wavy.

Finally she arrives and she has on a loose white skirt cut just above her knees, with a supertight white bodysuit type of blouse working the top. Damn, this girl is looking so fine with her hair draped all over her shoulders. Her lips are so big and full, they're filled out like a juicy plum about to burst from the rays of the sun, and they are naturally dark in color. I guess it's fair to say that she has a big mouth, literally, and I like it like that. Her eyes are super white, and they pierce me to the bone every time that she looks at me.

As we sit and talk to get better acquainted with each other, I see something in her beyond the surface. Damn, she has only been here for thirty minutes, so and if I tell her what I see in the future, she might think that I'm crazy or something. After I wait a few minutes, I can't resist telling her any longer. So I slowly reach out for her hands and hold the both of them gently as I look into her eyes and say, "Candy, you are going to be the mother of my daughter."

She immediately starts laughing at me because she thinks that this shit is so funny. She says, "Sergio, I am forty-one years old and I have two grown-ass boys at home, so I am definitely not trying to have nobody's baby. Where did that one come from anyway?" she says. "And why would you say something like that? You really know how to shock a lady, Sergio. I'll give you that," she says, as she continues to laugh at me. She's laughing so hard that she actually causes me to begin laughing with her.

She has no idea as to how serious I am until she stops laughing, and then I begin to prophesize. I tell her that I had been praying for a daughter for the past twenty years and that God has shown me that she is going to be the one to deliver her. I even go as far as describing her features, her gifts, and her talents. Candy is looking at me in amazement, but deep down inside I know that she believes me.

I explain to her that I am not expecting any specific reaction. I am just merely telling her now so that when it comes to pass, she will know that it was spoken. This is the first hour of the first date, and I've hit this girl with something she definitely wasn't expecting to hear. Surprisingly she took it all in well, and I'm quite happy about that.

As I look at her long golden-red legs, I can't help myself from imagining being between them. Unfortunately, I have to do my best at maintaining my composure and being at the best of my behavior. I only get one chance to make a first impression, and this is the first date, so I'm definitely not trying to go there sexually with her tonight.

After all, I'm not in that big of a hurry anyway, especially when I already know that she is going to be my girl. I'll have plenty of time for the sexual stuff later, but for now I must stimulate her mind. I need to find out more personal things about her, like what turns her on and what ticks her off. What type of goals does she have, and what is she doing to achieve them?

After a couple of dates, Candy and I begin to see each other on a regular basis. We never let a day go by without talking to each other. She usually comes over to my crib, but I have been to her apartment several times also. She has two sons: one is nineteen, and the other, twenty-three. The both of them are extremely tall; one is six foot five and the other is six foot seven. I've seen them play basketball, and the both of them can slam-dunk effortlessly.

Today I received a call from Candy, and she has a problem with the management in her apartment complex. Apparently, one of her son's visitors drove his car through the electric entrance gate last night and caused a significant amount of monetary damages to the property. Unfortunately, the meeting that she had with the property manager didn't go well, and now she wants to move as soon as possible.

I invite her to move in with me, being that she is there just about every night anyway. She gladly accepts my invite, and her sons will be coming along as well. This is going to be a challenge for me because I have never lived around two grown-ass kids before; however, I am willing to give this a try.

Months have passed and everything seems to be going well; actually, it's not as bad as I thought that it would be. Her sons totally respect me and my house, and we have been getting along just fine. Candy and I both work, so her sons have the house to themselves most of the day, and at night they are usually somewhere out in the streets.

I called her at work today, and she said that she has a surprise for me when I get home tonight. Now I'm all excited trying to figure out what it is. Could it be something sexy for her to wear and turn me on, perhaps, or did she buy me a gift of some sort? Either way, I must say that I am a little excited and I can't wait to get home tonight. If she has a surprise for me, then she is most likely going to make love to me later, and that's all good.

As soon as I step inside the door, she greets me with a kiss and a hug around my neck. The aroma of the dinner cooking on the stove is lurking all throughout the house, and she has the table set for only two people. She also has this radiant glow of happiness all over her face, and she's just standing there smiling at me without saying a word.

"Hey, baby, I'm glad to see that you're in a good mood, so what is the surprise that you have for me?" I ask. She says, "Close your eyes, Sergio, and don't peek." So I close my eyes and I don't peek, and then she says, "You can open your eyes up now."

When I open up my eyes, she is standing in front of me with her blouse pulled up to expose her stomach, and she then says, "I am pregnant, Sergio. We're going to have a baby."

"Oh shit, are you serious?" I ask. "Yes, I'm serious," she says. "You're the one that prophesized it months ago."

I immediately pick her up off her feet and spin her around the room, and she joyously shouts at me, "Put me down, Sergio! Put me down." Wow, I am so excited. I have been asking the Lord to bless me with a daughter for over twenty years. I don't need a doctor to tell me that it's a girl because I already know that she is exactly what I've prayed for.

Here I go again with a baby on the way, so I hope that I get the chance to raise the baby this time. I have been disappointed with death, abortion, and just plain old denial. I'm really looking forward to being a full-time father this time to my daughter; after all, I did pray for her for over twenty years.

I'm doing my best to make things as easy and comfortable for Candy as I possibly can. She insists on maintaining her job up until the last two months. I don't agree with her because she works as a security guard at a huge shopping mall. When she is not driving around the parking lot in the truck, she has to walk inside the mall. I personally think that she is spending too much time on her feet.

When I get home, I find joy in pampering her with home-cooked meals, candlelight bubble baths, foot rubs, and whatever else her little heart desires. We have a stable, trusting relationship with each other, and I try not to do anything that will stress her out or put that in jeopardy. We are in love with each other, and things couldn't be much better.

Months pass, and out of the blue I get a call from Peaches. After all this time, now she wants me to spend time with my son. That's all good because I would love to spend time with my son. It's just ironic that Peaches wouldn't allow me to pick him up before she found out that Candy is pregnant.

It seems to me that she may be a little jealous about the fact that I have moved on and that the Lord has blessed me with another child. One thing for sure is that she can't say that I screwed up the relationship between her and I. She and I both know that I did right by her, I loved her, and I treated her like a freaking queen.

When I arrive to pick up my son a couple of days later, she is dressed provocatively in an attempt to stimulate my sexual desire for her. I have to give it to her; she is looking pretty damn good. However, not good enough for me to risk what I have with Candy at home. I know that at the end of the day, my heart belongs to Candy, so I get my son and leave quickly.

My son is such a cute little kid, and everywhere that I stop with him, people come up to tell me how beautiful he is. Candy seems to have no problem with playing with him and feeding him. Surprisingly, she took him to the mall with her and bought him clothes and toys. I thought that was nice of her to do that, because I actually expected her to be a little jealous.

It's January 14, 2000, and finally Candy is in labor. I just got the phone call, and I am on my way to the hospital. Oh shit, the baby is almost here, and I am so excited. I have been waiting for this day for over twenty years, and finally she is here. Thank you, Jesus.

When I arrive at the hospital, the doctor tells me that there is a problem. She says that the baby is under a lot of stress because the cord is wrapped around her neck, and she must come out now. The doctor then advises me that she will be performing an emergency C-section in order to save the baby.

As I stand at Candy's head, looking over the sheet, I comfort her as I watch them cut her wide open with a laser. I look at her silently as if to say "Damn, don't you feel that shit? They are cutting you wide open, girl." Apparently, the shot that they gave her keeps her from feeling anything. After they cut her, the doctor opens her stomach up with some type of spreading device then reaches in and pulls my daughter out.

Damn, I've seen my son's natural birth, and now I've seen this birth. I must say that a woman is an amazing creature, and until a man experiences seeing something like this, he hasn't a clue as to how much power she has within her. A woman, without a doubt, is the moral fabric of family and love. It's a damn shame that most men don't appreciate their love and compassion.

How can a man not love a woman after watching her nourish and nurture his baby in the womb for nine months and then she gives birth to it right before his very eyes? I find this to be a moment that I will treasure for the rest of my life. No one can erase or take from me this experience of witnessing life being brought into existence.

My daughter is so beautiful, absolutely gorgeous, and I know that the Lord has equipped her with all the gifts and talents that I prophesized. This little girl is loaded, so look out, world, here she comes. After Candy and the baby get all cleaned up and settled into the hospital room, my mom and sister arrive.

My mom and sister compliment Candy on how good of a job she did with the baby and how beautiful she is. Then my mom passes me a Christmas gift that she had been saving for my son since the holidays that he hadn't picked up. It's a nice yellow leather jacket, and she asks me to give it to him the next time that I see him.

I can see it in Candy's eyes that she is pissed, so my mom and sister leave shortly afterward. Candy says, "Sergio, your mom didn't bring shit for your daughter. Instead she brings you something to take to your supposed son. Here I am lying here with her granddaughter, and she didn't so much as bring me a freaking card."

I'm literally speechless because I know that my mom didn't mean anything intentionally by bringing the gift, but on the other hand, I completely understand Candy's reaction. I can easily see how she took the scenario to be offensive. This is her day. So I look at her and say, "I'm sorry, baby, and I'm sure that my mom didn't mean anything negative by that, and yes, you are right, this is your day."

Once the baby is home, Candy and I have a discussion about her going back to work. I agree to her going back, on the condition that only a family member can babysit my daughter. The only way for that to happen is for me to have my job transferred to Tallahassee, Florida, and get a house there.

Candy's mom and sisters live in Thomasville, Georgia, which is only forty-five minutes away from Tallahassee. I don't want to be right up under her mother's nose, so a forty-five-mile trip will definitely do the trick. That way I can keep all of Candy's kin folks out of my business and won't have to put up with seeing them at my door every other day.

Two weeks later, Candy's mother comes to Atlanta from Thomasville for a weekend visit and to see her granddaughter. I tell her about our plans to move to Tallahassee, and then I give her the money to find a house for us to rent once she gets back. I give her enough to pay for first and last months' rent, electricity, gas, cable, water, and sewage services. I also paid her generously for her time and gas expenses that will be acquired.

Three weeks later, I find myself driving a moving truck heading to Tallahassee, Florida. Candy and the baby are in the BMW, and her brother is following behind in my Jeep Cherokee. We make a stop off in Thomasville first in order to see her mom and get the keys to the house that she rented for us.

Candy seems to be very happy about the fact that she is close to her family again, and they seem to be happy as well. Maybe this will work out just fine, being that my assistant store manager position at a major auto parts supplier was transferred. I have the crib, I have the job, I have two vehicles, and moreover, I have a beautiful woman that loves me and a beautiful baby.

The next day we leave the moving truck at her mother's house and take a ride to Tallahassee. We want to see the house so that we can decide on what colors that we want to use. We will probably stay at her mom's house for a week until I complete the painting and cleaning.

When I pull up in the driveway, I'm immediately satisfied with the size and location of the house and property. The house is fairly large with a two-car garage, and it's sitting on about an acre of land. I think that it's going to be more than enough space for the two of us and a baby.

Once we get inside, we find the place to be in fairly good shape. It has four bedrooms, two and a half bathrooms, kitchen, dining, living, and an extra entertainment room. The both of us like the house and think that Candy's mom made an excellent selection for us. I still want to paint the entire house before we move in, so it's off to the paint store I go.

It took us exactly six days to finish painting the house inside and out, and that was with additional help from her family. Finally I'm backing the moving truck up to the front door to unload our possessions, and it's the beginning of another big job that's going to take days to finish. Not so much the unloading, but the unpacking can be very time-consuming.

I haven't been in the house for two weeks yet, and my job is already sending me out of town for a week to attend a course in leadership. The company is paying for travel, food, and lodging, so it is absolutely mandatory for me to go if I want to remain employed. Candy and the baby will be staying at her mother's house until I return. I don't feel comfortable with them being home alone in a strange place.

After I return, we finally get a chance to enjoy the house with each other. It's such a joy sitting here watching my little baby run and play all over the house. This is worth working for, and this is what the meaning of life is all about. I am most happy with myself when those among me are happier.

Candy wanted to get a job, so I pulled a few strings with the company that I work for and got her a job delivering auto parts in Thomasville. I'm the assistant store manager at the Tallahassee location, and she's a driver at the Thomasville location. So sometimes the baby and her stay over in Thomasville for days at a time.

Six months later, I have a problem developing at my job with a certain coworker. She is a blond-haired, blue-eyed devil that keeps making little, small sexual gestures to me. Whenever she has to walk past me, she always gets close enough to brush up against me. I'm starting to get a little uncomfortable around her, and I think that she may possibly be trying to set me up.

It's the day before Valentine's Day, and she is the only employee in the store with me an hour before closing. There are literally no customers in the store, so I'm sitting behind the desk, admiring the gift that I bought for Candy. My coworker walks up to the desk and wants to know whom I bought the gift for. She seems to have some type of attitude about it, and I'm shocked at the way that she asked me.

Something is not right about this scenario, and I have a feeling that this is not the end of it. I play off her attitude as if I don't even know that she has one and try to finish out the hour before closing in a professional manner. I refuse to feed into whatever she's trying to accomplish through me, and I can see that she is plotting up in her head some shit to destroy me right now.

When I return to work two days after Valentine's Day, I can sense a change in the attitude of most of my coworkers. They seem to be a little distant from me. Two hours after my shift started, the regional manager walks in and pulls me into a meeting. I know this is not going to be good because it's just him and I.

He says, "Sergio, there has been a formal sexual harassment complaint filed against you by a coworker. She says that you have asked her to go out with you, and now she's uncomfortable working under your supervision. I'm sorry," he says. "But I am going to have to ask you for the keys to the store and suspend you pending our investigation."

I just look at that dude for a couple of seconds without saying a word so that I can swallow what he just said to me. He's a freaking redneck, and this is pleasurable for him. So I'm not going to give him the satisfaction of letting him feel that he just crushed my world. I stand up proudly and pass him the keys and say, "It seems to me that you have already concluded your investigation without talking to me."

As I drive away, I start to replay in my mind all the little moves that little white girl tried to put on me and didn't work. I knew that she was bad news, but I didn't expect her to go this far. Oh well, I guess I'll have to find a job turning wrenches again. I can always fall back on my auto technician skills, and fortunately, I brought all my tools here.

I try to look at every change as progress, instead of being fearful, sitting around pouting about it. So I'll just look at the positive aspect of it. Actually I can make more money and work less hours when I work on cars. I won't have to close the store at night anymore and take the risk of being robbed or killed. I won't have to work on weekends anymore, so I can spend more time with my family. Looking at the situation from that perspective puts being suspended in a whole different light.

Two days later I apply for a technician job at an independent shop, and not only does he hire me on the spot, but he also hires me as his service manager and gives me complete control. I have three technicians and one general service tech that works under my direct supervision.

The building is absolutely huge. I hired Candy as my assistant, and I have an office set up for her and the baby. The office is so big that it is large enough for me to set up an area for the baby to have her own little nursery inside it. Candy is able to take care of the baby as she works, and of course, sometimes I have the baby as well. It's a great setup, and I wouldn't trade it for my previous job as a parts store manager.

The building is on a huge piece of property, maybe twenty acres or more. The owner of the property rents out about two acres of his land to a trailer home company. On one side of the rental space, they have brand-new furnished units parked for storage. On the other side of the space they have abandoned and semidemolished units parked as well.

After working here for six months, the weather has changed from warm to extremely hot in Tallahassee. My employer asked me to go inside one of the trashed trailers and remove a blower unit from the wall. He wants to use the circular fan unit inside the shop to generate more airflow for the technicians.

While inside the trailer, I discover a cordless drill, an old bookshelf, an old desk, and a chair made of wood. I decided to take them all home with me and make a project out of restoring them. With the help of the technicians, I loaded up one piece per day until I had them all at the house.

I worked relentlessly on the pieces by sanding the surfaces, staining the wood, and finally applying the gloss coat for the finish. They are absolutely beautiful, if I must say so myself. As I bring everything into the room that I have especially for them, I can then appreciate all the work that I have put into them. While sitting behind the empty but beautiful desk, I stop and exhale. At that very moment I have a vision of writing a book.

I have no idea as to what I could possibly write a book about, but I have seen the vision of it coming to pass. The devil still attacks me in my dreams with crazy shit concerning death and pain, and I always wake up in the nick of time. The Lord, on the other hand, shows me visions of things to come, so maybe I'll write about that one of these days.

My little baby girl is starting to walk and talk a little bit, and it is such a joy watching her take those first steps and say those first words. Even though I am around her all through the day while at work, it's not the same as that one-on-one time we share when we are at home. This little girl is my world, and I put no one before her but God himself.

A couple of weeks later, the owner of the busted up trailer comes on the property for the first time that I have ever seen. He's talking to the owner of the property about someone going inside his unit and taking furniture. I overhear the conversation and admit to having the furniture at my house, and I also offer to return it.

I try to explain to the guy that I thought it was all trash. The unit is literally falling apart, so I wrongfully assumed that the contents of it are all trash too. I also tell him that I have restored everything and would be more than happy to return it to him. He's looking at me like I am the scum of the earth, and he wouldn't dare lose out on the opportunity to lock my black ass up.

This guy is a redneck, and my employer is in complete denial of his participation in the matter, mostly because the guy is not concerned with the structural damage as he is about the contents removed. Damn, this is going to be some shit over this abandoned little desk and shelf. Now I have to go home and worry about when are the freaking police coming to my door.

The next morning I wake up tired because I didn't get much sleep last night. I was up half the night worrying about what's going to happen concerning the office furniture. I manage to pull myself together and make it to work, but shortly thereafter, a detective calls me on the shop phone.

"Sergio, did you take some items from a trailer at your place of employment?" she asks. "Yes, I did, ma'am, but I thought it was trash," I reply. "I need you to come down and give me a statement," she says. "Are you going to arrest me?" I ask. "No," she replies, "I just need you to give me a statement."

I go inside the police station, nervous as hell, not knowing whether or not I would be walking back out. I meet up with the detective and give her the story as to how the office furniture ended up at my house, and I tell her the absolute truth. The only thing that I didn't tell her is who helped me move it, and she commended me for not snitching.

She allowed me to freely walk back out of the door, and she said that she would get in touch with me to let me know what the owner wants me to do with the furniture. I'm relieved to be able to go back to my family. As soon as I get back inside the house, I pick up my daughter and hold her tightly, because that was a close call for me to be taken away from her.

Thirty days later the detective finally calls me and tells me that the owner of the furniture wants me to put it back inside the trailer. I tell her to give me three days to put it back because it took me three days to get it out. She agrees and says, "Just call me when everything is back inside, and I will come and check it all off."

It's Friday afternoon pouring down rain, and I finally got the last piece of furniture back inside the trailer. Candy, the baby, and I are going to Atlanta today as soon as we get off work, but first I must call the detective to come out and check everything off.

I can see the detective coming down the road to the shop in an unmarked police car; she is being followed by a deputy sheriff. This does not look good. Why would she need a squad car behind her? After checking everything off her list, she looks at me and says, "Sergio, this furniture looks absolutely gorgeous."

She then says, "I'm sure that it didn't look this good when you removed it from the trailer. You have been a man of your word," she says. "But unfortunately, the owner of the property took out a warrant for your arrest, so I'm going to have to take you in."

"Oh shit, are you freaking kidding me?" I ask. "I'm sorry, Sergio, but no, I am not kidding you, so would you do me a favor and interlock your fingers on the top of your head for me please." While being body-searched before they handcuff me, I ask, "Exactly what am I being charged with?"

She says, "Sergio, you are being charged with two felony counts of grand theft, two felony counts of burglary of structure, and two felony counts of defrauding a pawnshop."

"Six freaking felonies over a piece of trash that I restored and returned, are you freaking serious?" I ask.

Candy and I both have tears in our eyes as she holds the baby and watches the deputy put me in the backseat of his patrol car. As I am sitting in the back of the car, handcuffed, reality sets in as the deputy pulls into the jail. Lord, help me, please. I don't want to be taken away from my family.

During the booking process, I requested to be in a cell all by myself, and what a big mistake that turned out to be because they put me straight in the hole. I have been placed in a secluded area, and it's dark and cold here. I can feel the presence of the devil all around me; this place is evil, and I'm sitting right in the middle of it.

After two days of darkness with no food and shower, I'm starting to feel like an animal, and I have no idea as to what time of day or night it is. The devil has been having his way with my mind, because being in the dark like this is like being in a bad dream that you don't wake up from. I feel as if it's just me against the world. Where is your god now, and what did you do to deserve this treatment? Those are the questions that the devil keeps asking me over and over.

Finally they pull me out of the hole and put me in another cell all by myself. It's dark inside this cell as well, and the little, small window has been painted so that I can't see the outside world. They allow me fifteen minutes outside the cell to take a shower only three times a week, and they slide my food through a trapdoor like I'm a freaking serial killer or something.

I am surrounded by serious criminals. The guy in the cell directly across mine executed someone in the streets in broad daylight. The guy in the cell next to him has all his clothes off, and he is literally spreading his own shit all over himself. When the officer comes to get him out of the cell, he then tries to put shit all over him as well. I've seen some crazy things before, but this surpasses all because this guy is insane.

Four days later, Candy comes to visit me, and she is highly upset as to why they have me isolated from the general population. She and I both have tears falling from our eyes as she looks at me through the glass window. I'm glad that she didn't bring my daughter here because I don't want her to see me caged like an animal. Furthermore, I don't want her near all these evil spirits lurking around.

I don't know whom Candy raised hell with, but two days later, they move me into a cell with another inmate in general population. This guy is about ten years younger than I, and he will most likely never see the streets as a free man again. He's being charged with murder, and his sentence will be life in prison.

After being in the cell with him for three weeks, he opens up and tells me all the details of how and why he killed a guy. I tried several times to discourage him from telling me because I really didn't want to know that much information about his case. It must be eating him up inside, because he insists on venting to me.

He says that he was propositioned to do the hit by a gang of dope boys from the MIA. The hit was on his very own supplier; this is the guy that he had been buying his package from for years. He says, "Damn, Sergio, the guy trusted me. That's the only reason that I was able to get that close to him for a close-range shot."

I continue to sit up on the bottom bunk in silence, as he lies across the top bunk and let it all out. He says, "Sergio, an hour before I went to kill this guy, the gang was playing the song 'Life' by K-Ci and JoJo over and over again. Now that song keeps ringing in my freaking head nonstop, because that's exactly what the courts are going to give me."

He says that they put a plate full of cocaine in front of him and told him to help himself to as much as he wanted. After snorting cocaine and listening to that song over and over for an hour, he was ready to do the job. Then he says that once he made entry into the house, less than two minutes later, he had put a bullet in the guy's head from point-blank range.

He continues and says, "Damn, Sergio, as soon as I ran out the door into the parking lot, the police was right there waiting on me with their weapons drawn. The dope boys from the MIA wanted my supplier dead so that they could take over his established drug turf. They were going to pay me a stack and a half ounce of cocaine to do the job. Look at me now," he says. "I'm twenty-four years old and I will never walk the streets as a free man again, ever."

Even though I know that he is guilty of taking another man's life, I still have a sense of compassion for him. When I think about the fact that he will never walk the streets as a free man again, it bothers me. On the other hand, when I think about the life that he has taken and the family that he has affected, he deserves exactly what he is getting.

After sitting back silently for a week or so just observing all the other inmates around me, I discern whom to associate with and whom not to. There's this one particular guy within our pod that keeps looking at me and inviting me to join him and a group of guys in Bible study. He is actually a minister of his own church on the outside, but he committed a crime like the rest of us and he's here facing charges.

He continually tells me that there's something special about my spirit. He also says that he recognizes that I have some spiritual gifts, and he wants me to join him in study and prayer. It really doesn't take much of a push for me when the subject matter is concerning Jesus, so I decide to join them in their study of the Word.

Within the first half hour of the study, we stop and the minister begins to pray. As he is praying, the Holy Spirit comes upon me and I do my best to contain it within me. To no avail, the spirit overpowers me and I'm speaking in tongues in front of the entire pod of inmates. When the spirit finally releases me and I open my eyes, everyone is silent and looking at me as if they have never seen someone speak in tongues before.

The minister breaks the silence by saying, "I knew it, I knew all along that you had the Holy Ghost in you, Sergio. The Lord has a major plan and purpose for your life." He says, "And he is going to bring a blessing on you large enough to affect a lot of people." Every inmate in the pod is looking at me with a new sense of respect, and they know that I'm under a hedge of protection from the Lord.

Finally, after forty-five days of being locked up and facing five years of prison time, my court date comes up. The Lord sends me the oldest and most respected public defender in the county to represent me in court. After him pulling a few strings and doing what he does best, the attorney gets me out of jail. My sentence is two years of probation time with a three-thousand-dollar fine.

When they finally called me out of the pod to be released, I couldn't be happier than at that very moment. The Holy Spirit enters the holding cell with me as I change back into my street clothes, and I begin to get in the spirit. As I sit there uttering in tongues, my grandmother's spirit manifests itself right before my very eyes. She tells me that she loves me and that she will always be watching over me.

The next day I report to the probation office so that I can get everything transferred to Atlanta. I don't want to stay in Tallahassee any longer because things have not gone well for me here. After I spend almost all day waiting to get the approval from my probation officer, he, unfortunately, gives me the bad news that he can't get my probation transferred out of the state.

"Oh shit, you mean to tell me that I have to stay in this state for two years?" I ask. "Yes," he says, "you can't leave the state of Florida without my permission, or you will violate your probation." Now I'm really frustrated. I have just been released from jail, and I feel like they still have me in bondage.

After thinking about the situation for a moment, I come up with another idea. I ask the probation officer if he can transfer my probation to another county within the state, and he says yes. I explain to him that I have no family and friends in Tallahassee, so it would be a huge problem with me finding employment and housing at this point. He, fortunately, agrees to transfer my probation to Lake County, Florida, where my dad lives. So now I'm going to have to go back there again to fulfill my obligations.

Candy is upset about the situation because she knows that this is going to keep us apart a little longer. Now I have to go all the way back down to Tavares, get a job, and get a place to stay. Damn, I have a lot on my plate right now, and I'm worried about what's up ahead for me and my family. I guess I'll deal with it as it comes, but for now I'm going straight to Georgia to see my baby girl.

As I cross over the state line without permission, heading straight to Thomasville to see my daughter, I look over at Candy and say, "Damn them crackers. I have been sitting in jail for almost two months, so there is nothing going to stop me from seeing my baby girl today." She looks over at me and smiles, and then she says, "I know that's right, Sergio."

Probation

Three days later, after spending all my time with Candy and the baby in Thomasville, I find myself back in Tavares at my dad's house. Candy and the baby are here with me, and they will be staying a couple of days before returning to Atlanta. She has agreed to come back and live with me here as soon as I get everything situated, so I guess it won't be that bad after all. I am happy no matter where I am, just as long as I have her and the baby by my side.

A week later, Candy and the baby returns to Atlanta, so now it's time for me to get on the grind and make something happen. I start by applying for an auto technician position at every dealership in Lake County. As I look around the shops during the process, I can't find even one black auto technician at any of the dealerships.

I have twenty years of experience as an auto technician, six ASE certifications, and five years of experience in management. Everywhere that I apply for a job, these crackers are intimidated by my knowledge and experience. Furthermore, they do not want to pay a nigga that kind of money regardless of my talents and skills.

After a couple of weeks of being told that I am overqualified for the job, I'm forced to go to plan B on these crackers. I refuse to let their rejection get the best of me and hold me back from being able to take care of my family. My dad has a service truck sitting in the yard that he used for his old tire service business, so I'm going to put it back on the road and use it to do mobile auto repair.

I start by going to the print shop and getting myself some business cards made. Once I have the business cards in hand, I start hanging out at different auto parts stores, passing them out to potential customers. After about a month of promoting myself to people face-to-face, I begin to start getting work. Before long, I have so much work that my customers have to make appointments in order for me to get to them.

After a couple of weeks pass with my business starting to flourish, the Lord blesses me with renting the property next door to my dad. The lady that lives there also has a home in Michigan, so every summer when it's hot, she goes up north, and she returns to Florida when it's cold. The two-acre property has a house and a two-bedroom trailer sitting on it, so she's letting me live in the trailer.

Before I move into the trailer, I decide to completely remodel it inside and out. So now I'm spending countless hours and a lot of money trying to get it nice enough for Candy and the baby to be comfortable. I start by changing all the flooring inside to hardwood floors. Yes, you heard it right, hardwood floors in a freaking trailer. The next task is applying the most beautiful and expensive wallpapers that Home Depot has to offer, on the walls.

I'm also restoring all the natural woodwork in the kitchen and replacing the sink and appliances. The bathroom will be completely remodeled as well, because I don't want to leave even one stone unturned inside this freaking trailer.

Finally after finishing the inside, I painted the outside as well and did all the landscaping on the property. Damn, after a month of working continually on this shit with no help, I'm ready for Candy and the baby to join me. I have bought furniture, linen, cookware, and all the other necessities needed for a comfortable home.

A week later, Candy and the baby arrive, and she brought her grandbaby with her as well. Her grandbaby is only four months younger than our daughter, and she's a bundle of joy just like our daughter. Candy wants her to stay awhile so that she can experience the joy of Disney World and the beaches, and I couldn't be happier than I am right now. I have the woman that I love, my daughter, and the grandbaby all here with me, God is so good.

I kick things off by taking them to Disney World to see all the cartoon characters that they have seen on television. They are so excited and happy, and I'm doing my best to spoil the both of them rotten. My daughter has a lot of my ways in her character; she does not trust rides, she does not like heights, and she definitely doesn't trust people. The grandbaby, on the other hand, is the complete opposite of her; she's a little daredevil.

Wow, I'm having so much fun with these two little girls. I know that the grandbaby has to go back home to her mother, and when she does, it's going to leave me melancholic. I have become quite attached to her, and I love her almost as much as I love my own daughter. I did say almost as much, for no one walking the face of this earth means more to me than my daughter.

Every day after I finish work, I try to do something exciting with them, whether it be going out or staying in. When I wake up every morning, my objectives for the day are to make money and to make Candy and the kids happy. My felicity comes from seeing them happy. If they are good, then so am I.

The following weekend I take them to Daytona Beach, and they are just as excited about the beach as they were about Disney World. My daughter loves the water and the waves, but she will not go any farther than ankle-deep, and that's with me holding her hand. This little girl is so smart. She says, "Daddy, I can't see what's in that water."

Even when I pick her up and try to walk out in the water to my waist, she says, "Daddy, turn around and go back, because something might get us." I can only smile at her and hold her tightly because she is so right; there is that possibility. Not only that, but I know she got that don't-take-chances shit from me. While we walk along the beach, picking up shells, Candy and the grandbaby are tripping on letting the waves hit them from their back and knocking them over time and time again.

The next day I have to report to the probation office, and I hate having to go there. It's like once a month there's a possibility that I may be going back to jail. Actually, if I get arrested for any reason, I will be going to prison for the first time. I'm nervous every time that I step in that office because I still smoke weed.

I spent fifty dollars on an antitoxicant drink that is supposed to clean my system out from any drug. I always stop smoking weed a week before it's time for me to report, in order to give my body time to cleanse. I drink two gallons of water per day for five days prior to walking in the probation office, and so far I have been coming up clean.

In all reality, even though I take the necessary precautions, I know that it ultimately depends on the Lord. I always pray a prayer before walking into that office, and I know that my prayers to God are what miraculously sustain me. Sometimes my probation officer doesn't ask me to take a urine test, and on those days I know that it's the power of God that tells her to leave me alone.

Every time that I walk out of that office, I pray as soon as I get back into my car. Before I put the key in the ignition and start the engine, the spirit of the Lord always comes and comforts me. So here I am parked on Main Street in the middle of downtown, crying and speaking in tongues in broad daylight.

A week later it's time for the grandbaby to go back to Atlanta, and I am surely going to miss her. Candy and my daughter will be returning within a week, so I'll be looking forward to that. In the meantime, I'm focusing on getting some of my work caught up. I have been spending a lot of money lately, so now it's time to restore my little in-house bank.

My dad and stepmother live next door, and they have been very supportive concerning my family. My stepmother is a very soft-spoken woman that has an intimate relationship with God. Periodically I go next door to sit and talk with her about the Word. She is full of the Holy Ghost, and I love to have discussions with her about life in general.

My dad, on the other hand, is still a player. He leaves her home alone every Friday and Saturday night, just as he did with my mother in Atlanta. He is so predictable, and I know that she is aware of his cheating. Sometimes I feel sorry for her because I know that she hides her true pain behind that lovely smile that she carries on her face all the time.

She has been working for the same hospital for forty years, and she hates to miss a day of work. She also attends church at least three times a week, and I have never seen her angry or heard a bad word come from her mouth. I love her almost as much as I love my real mother, and she knows it too. Sometimes I get very angry with my dad because I don't like the way that he treats her.

Candy and my daughter are on their way back from Atlanta. She just called me and said that the car has broken down on her approximately fifty miles south of Macon. They are waiting for me to pick them up from a gas station just off the exit. Damn, I don't want them to be there at night all alone because she says that the station will be closing in four hours.

I quickly attach the car dolly to the truck and proceed to head out. Once I get on Interstate 75, I put the pedal to the metal, trying to get there as soon as I can. I'm doing a hundred miles per hour and I'm not even thinking about a freaking police. If I get caught driving this fast, surely it will violate my probation, but I have to take the risk. I am not going to have them sitting there all alone at night no longer than they have to be, so I put my trust and faith in God.

Four hours later I'm there, and the gas station is just about to close. They are so glad to see me, and the feeling is mutual. I wouldn't be able to forgive myself if something happened to them. As soon as I loaded the car on to the dolly, the lights at the gas station were turned off. I literally made it just in time; if it had taken me just a few minutes longer, they would have been in the dark in a vulnerable situation.

Finally, after driving eight straight hours, I'm back at the crib. My daughter has never slept in her own room and in her own bed, so I'm very optimistic as to that happening soon. I'm going to have to wean her off sleeping with Candy, and I know that's going to take some time. She is so scary that sometimes it's funny.

I know that she's a dreamer like me because sometimes when I watch her, she laughs and cries while she's asleep. Just like they did when I was a youngster, the devil and God are having a battle for her very soul. She is gifted like me as well, so the devil is already messing with her while she dreams. Candy gets angry every time that she sees her cry while she's asleep. Then all of a sudden, the angels come and play with her and make her laugh again.

My daughter is inevitably going to be a spiritual force to be reckoned with. I prayed for her existence for more than twenty years, and I know that God installed in her all the right ingredients for success. She is nothing short of an angel in disguise, and I'm going to do everything that I can to make sure that the manifestation of her power is not hindered.

There is no sweeter sound to my ears than the sound of her calling me Daddy. She can get anything that she wants from me within reason, and I make damn sure that she knows that I love her. Not only do I tell her that every day, but I also do my best to show her that every day. I make sure that she and I spend quality time with each other daily to strengthen our bond, and no one is going to be able to break it.

Candy, on the other hand, I'm not so sure about. I love her and I do everything that I can to keep her happy, but at times I feel like her heart is not in the relationship. Only time will tell whether or not we make this last, but one thing that I do know for sure is that I can't make this work all by myself. I can love her until I turn blue in the face, but if she doesn't truly love me back, then it is what it is.

Sometimes I feel like she's more concerned about her grown-ass boys in Atlanta than she is about our daughter. In the beginning of our relationship, she was respectful, kind, and honest, but now she's becoming to be a mean, ungrateful bitch. I think that my love for her is solely based on her being the mother of my daughter. Otherwise, I don't think that I would be with her at all.

She has such a foul mouth and an evil attitude, and the more that I am around her, the more it rubs off on me. She and I have never sat down together and had a discussion about the Bible. As a matter of fact, I have never heard her say the name Jesus. We are definitely not equally yoked, and I wonder at times why God picked her to have my little angel.

My daughter doesn't look anything like her; she looks just like me. Neither does she have her personality; it's just like mine also. The only two attributes that I can see come from her mother are her beautiful long hair and her height. Candy is still holding a grudge against my mom from the scenario that happened at my daughter's birth, and now she wants me to disclaim my son by Peaches.

I don't understand why she's so adamant about me denying my son, being that it takes nothing away from my daughter. I think that she is bothered by the fact that my son has a light skin tone and my daughter doesn't. The both of them are beautiful kids, so why should that even matter? Whenever we get into an argument, that is usually the first thing that she throws in my face.

"That's not your son," she says. "How can two black-ass niggas have a light-skinned baby?" Peaches is not dark; she has a caramel skin tone. However, she is a little darker than Candy, so I guess that's the reason Candy doesn't believe it's my son. She doesn't understand that God can do whatever he wants to do. He could've made my son green if he wanted to.

A couple of weeks later, Candy wants to go to Atlanta for the weekend. I have work to do here, so she and my daughter have to make the trip without me. The Nissan Maxima that I bought for her is still sitting in the backyard with a busted transmission, and it's a damn shame how she dogged that car out. It was in excellent condition when I gave it to her, but now it's a piece of shit.

Reluctantly I pull out my BMW 535i and tell her that she can drive it to Atlanta. Two days after she leaves, I get a phone call from her son, and he says that they were just involved in an accident. "Oh shit, is everybody all right?" I ask. He says that Candy, my daughter, and the grandbaby are all in the hospital.

Damn, I immediately hang the phone up and jump in the truck to head for Atlanta right away. When I get to the hospital and see Candy, she is all messed up with cracked ribs, a head injury, and a busted knee. Her face is so swollen that her eyes are almost completely closed, and she is barely recognizable. My daughter and the grandbaby only have a couple of scratches, so I'm relieved to know that they are all right. As soon as I entered the room, both of them got out of bed and jumped in my arms for me to hold them.

My daughter looks at me and says, "Daddy, that really scared me." I kiss her forehead and reply, "I know that scared you, baby, but everything is going to be all right." Then I ask her if anything hurts her besides her nose, and she says, "No, Daddy, I'm just scared." The grandbaby, on the other hand, is laughing about the accident, and she says, "Sergio, that car hit us so hard, it went *boom!*"

I needed that laugh, and I'm glad that somebody has a sense of humor. My daughter is as girly as a girl can be, and she is very sensitive about her prissy little self. The grandbaby is totally the opposite of my daughter. She is tough as nails and has a tomboyish personality. Even still, I ask her as well if anything hurts her, and she replies, "No, Sergio, I'm not hurt."

My daughter became an aunt when she was only four months old, and I know that seems crazy, but it is what it is. I know that sometimes she wonders why the grandbaby calls me Sergio and she is not allowed to call me that. It's because I'm not married to Candy, so technically she is not my grandbaby. That's the only reason that I allow her to call me Sergio.

After talking to Candy's son, I find out exactly how the accident happened. She had been drinking most of the day and evening, so she was well intoxicated. As a matter of fact, the police smelled alcohol on her and found several empty beer cans inside the car.

They also found excessive toxicants in her blood and say that she was extremely hostile. The police left three traffic tickets for her at the hospital, so she was definitely in the wrong. They stated that she tried to make a left turn in front of oncoming traffic and was hit right under the traffic light.

I don't want her to get upset, so I don't even mention the fact that the police left three tickets for her downstairs in the property room. She looks bad and I know that she is in pain, so I don't want to make a bad situation worse by telling her that she has tickets downstairs. For now all I can do is try to comfort her and stay by her side. The hospital actually let me sleep inside the room with her for three nights, and I think that's very considerate on their part.

The next day I go out to see my car and the amount of damage that was done. As soon as I laid eyes on it, I fell to my knees and thanked the Lord for allowing them to live. It's freaking unbelievable that no one was killed; the car is totaled. It was hit at the right front fender, and the impact was so hard that it caused some very extensive damage.

The steering wheel is on the floorboard, and instead of the gear selector pointing north and south, it is pointing east and west. The air-conditioning compressor is broken completely away from the engine, and the entire front half of the car is twisted to the left. The windshield is completely obliterated, and the passenger seat is positioned in the middle of the car. Ironically, the only thing that is not disturbed is the Holy Bible that I have sitting in the back glass. It didn't even move from the place that I put it.

When I returned to the hospital, Candy's sister had arrived from Thomasville. She pulled me to the side and pleaded with me to take Candy back to Florida with me. At first I wondered why she was doing that, because I had every intention to take her back anyway. Then all of a sudden, it dawned on me. Candy has a drug and alcohol problem; that's why her sister wants me to take her away.

Now I understand why she wanted to come back in the first place—not so much to see her sons, but in essence it was because she wanted to get high. I'm not talking about getting high on weed, because I smoke weed daily. I think she's getting high on crack cocaine, along with becoming a freaking alcoholic as well.

I keep my thoughts on the down low and decide just to be more observant concerning her behavior. After she is released from the hospital, I take her and my daughter back to Florida so that she can recover from her injuries. The doctor said that it will take a couple of months for her to completely heal, so now it's my job to take care of her.

For a couple of months, I have been doing everything that I possibly can to help her healing process. After I finish my work for the day, I always go straight home to cook, clean, and whatever else that needs to be done to make her happy and comfortable. It seems that no matter what I do for her, she is still not satisfied and she wants to go back to Atlanta.

One evening after working a full eight-hour day and returning home, I walk into the door and find out that she has left me. She had her brother come from Thomasville to pick her up and take her back to Atlanta. Man, I can't believe she did this shit; what an ungrateful bitch she is. Not to mention that she has taken the one thing that means more to me than anything in this world. This bitch has taken my daughter away from me.

I've been hurt by a woman before, but nothing compares to this because my daughter is involved. That is my blessing, not hers, and I'm the one that prayed for twenty years to bring forth that manifestation, not Candy. She is my gift from God, so why did he allow this to happen to me? This is the third child that has been snatched out of my hands, not to mention the twins that Mango aborted at five months and the daughter that I lost in Strawberry's sack.

What in the hell is going on, and what's up with that? The very thing that a lot of men take for granted is the very thing that I can't seem to accomplish no matter how hard I try. I am devastated and my stepmom knows it, so she comes over and tries her best to console me.

She says, "Sergio, I have been sitting back watching you, and, son, you have done everything that a man supposed to do, and then some. I know that you are crazy about that little girl and it hurts, but you're going to be all right." As I look at her, I can't hold it in any longer, so the tears start flowing from my eyes like the running waters of a river.

Crack

Candy and my daughter have been gone for three months now, and I still get depressed every time that I go into my daughter's bedroom. Tonight I have company, so I locked the door closed to avoid questions about the room. I don't want my company to see how beautiful the room is and then start asking me questions about my daughter.

Anyway, I just met this pretty little white girl, so I don't want her snooping around the place. Her name is Snow, and she's only twenty-eight years old. This girl is fine and extremely cute with her blond hair and blue eyes. When I look at her, I think about the phrase that Minister Louis Farrakhan uses, "She's a blue-eyed devil."

Yes, indeed, a blue-eyed devil is exactly what she is, because she has only been in my crib for ten minutes and she's already taking her clothes off and pulling out her crack pipe. Damn, crack cocaine does not discriminate; it doesn't give a shit how pretty you are. If you hit it, then you belong to it. Snow is filling my tub up with hot water and bubbles, and she wants to smoke her crack while sitting in my tub. Strange but cool. I'm due for a little excitement of some sort.

After sitting there for five minutes looking at her wet body dripping water and suds, I pick up the freaking pipe and get that first blast. Ooh shit, damn, I am so freaking high, man. I'm trying to talk, but there is no sound coming out of my mouth, and my heart is beating as fast as a freaking hummingbird's.

This is more than just getting high; this shit takes over the spirit. I have never at any point and time felt that the Lord wasn't inside me, until now. It feels as if the crack is associated with the devil, because I have no desire to do anything positive. I feel ashamed, dirty, and changed, so I don't want anyone to see me this way.

After ten or fifteen minutes of tripping, the sensation starts to decrease and now I want another hit of crack cocaine. Damn, this shit is so addictive that I literally spend every dollar in my pocket to continue to smoke the rest of the night. In between smoking, Snow entertains me with sexual favors for letting her continue to smoke with me.

The next morning I can still feel the effects of the drug physically, emotionally, and most of all, spiritually. As I look into the mirror, I notice that my face doesn't look the same, so now it's going to take me another day just to recoup. The after effects are just as bad as the actual smoking, because now I feel dirty and unworthy of God.

Not only that, I definitely can't leave out the fact that while smoking crack, it can possibly kill you at any given time that you hit it. The rush of the high can give you a heart attack if you are not careful. Even being careful doesn't eliminate you from the vulnerability of being killed by the drug; it could happen at any moment.

Two days later I'm finally back to normal, and now I have to catch up on the two days that I have missed from working. I still get my respect and dignity in the streets because no one even suspects me of smoking crack. I carry myself like a professional should at all times when I'm out here in the streets and talking to people about their vehicles.

I would never want any of my customers to know that I had smoked some crack. I'm pretty sure that would change the way that they think and feel about me. As a matter of fact, I wouldn't be able to do this type of job high on crack even if I wanted to anyway. I'm a mobile auto technician, so that involves driving, public relations, also diagnostics and repairs of vehicles.

Shit, when I'm high on crack, I don't want to move from wherever I am; it's like I'm stuck. In my mind I know that it's wrong, so I'm afraid of the police arresting me, and I'm also ashamed of someone seeing me all bug-eyed on the drug. Either way it would be an embarrassing scenario for me to deal with, so I don't take the chance of leaving the house while I'm all beamed up.

A week later, I have three women in the crib at the same time. It's amazing how much power this drug has, because I used it to lure all three of them here. I don't like to get high all alone because I think that the drug is too dangerous to do that. So I invited all three them here to smoke with me and keep me company.

Now even though I have them in a vulnerable situation by being in control of the flow of the drug, I'm still not going to try to take advantage of them. I'm going to give each one of them the most ultimate amount of respect as a woman, and I'm definitely not going to ask them to do anything that's immoral.

Before the daylight catches me, I make sure that everyone disappears from my crib. The last thing that I need is for people to start labeling my crib as a crack house, so I don't plan on doing that shit here again. Actually, I think from now on I'm going to go to this little spot I know that's about ten miles away from here.

There's this cute petite girl that lives four houses down from where I go to cop my dope. She has invited me to stop by there several times, so I think that I'll take her up on that offer. She's black, but she has a white husband, and he smokes crack as well. She told me that I could stop by there at any time and it wouldn't matter if her husband was there are not, so the next time that I go cop some dope, I'm going to see what's up.

Damn, these months are going by so fast because before you know it, it's time for me to report to my probation officer again. I'm always nervous when I go there, but this time I'm actually scared. If my probation officer finds cocaine in my system, she will surely violate me, and that means I will have to do five years of prison time.

For me to take a risk like this while being fully aware of the consequences, I have to be addicted. As soon as I walk into her office, she gives me a urine test cup and tells me to wait for a male officer to escort me to the bathroom. He is supposed to stand there and watch me urinate in the cup, but strangely enough he walks out of the bathroom to answer his cell phone.

Once he walks out of the bathroom, I immediately start looking for a way to cheat the test. The water in the toilet is blue, so I definitely can't dilute my urine with that. I have no other choice but to use the sink water, even though I'm worried about whether or not they will hear me turn it on.

After finishing filling the cup, I come out of the bathroom and pass it to my probation officer. She can't determine whether it's positive or negative,so she gets an opinion from another officer. The other officer comes in and looks at the test, then he looks at me, he looks at the test again, and then he looks at me and says, "He's clean. The test is negative."

Whew, now that was close, very close. If I hadn't diluted my urine with the sink water, I would've failed that drug test for sure. Damn, I need to kick myself in the ass for putting myself under that much pressure. This shit doesn't make any sense. I'm risking everything just to smoke some freaking crack.

Now that I feel like the weight of the world has been lifted off my shoulders. I foolishly prepare myself to go and get high again. Even though I realize that it was the power of God that just saved me from going to prison, I'm still headed straight to the devil's advocate to buy some more crack cocaine.

As I pull up to the dope house, I stop and think about the scripture Romans 7:15. I then whisper silently to heaven, "Help me, Jesus. I really don't want to do this, but the sinful nature within my body has an appetency for the drug." For the first time, I'm admitting to myself that I have a problem, and I know that at this point I can only be saved by Jesus Christ.

After I get the dope, I go straight down the street to see the girl that invited me to come over at any given time. She's very happy to see me because she knows that I just bought a package and she wants to smoke. Fortunately, her husband is not at home today and he won't be back until tomorrow, so everything is definitely going to be on and popping.

Weeks pass and I have been turning this little girl out. I go to her house at least three times a week, and every time that I go there, we get high together. She wants me to have sex with her, but I continue to turn her down, reason being is because I don't have any feelings for her. She is only just a trick for me, and I don't do tricks. The only thing that I allow her to do is oral sex, and of course I wear protection when she does that.

I never touch her in any type of way because I have to be emotionally stimulated in order for that to happen. She can be sitting right in front of me with no clothes on, and I still won't touch her. Even when I'm high on crack cocaine, nothing seems to penetrate that barrier. It's a simple strategy, yet it's very effective. If I don't have any love for you, then I will definitely not enter you. I know that may sound weird, but I still have some morals left in my character.

A couple of days later on my way home from working, I run into this pretty little white girl that I've had my eyes on for weeks. Periodically, I see her driving by, and I've been telling myself that I'm going to get her. She looks like a little schoolteacher with her glasses on, and she appears to be a very intelligent and virtuous woman.

She's smiling at me as I walk up to her to introduce myself, and her eyes are fixated on my body as she looks at me up and down. Immediately she introduces herself by saying, "Hi, my name is Dina," and she wastes no time on giving me her telephone number. She also tells me that she has seen me around before and that she was very interested in getting to know me just as well.

A couple of hours later, after I finished cleaning up from working, I called her up, and surprisingly she wants to come over to see me tonight. When she arrives, she has on a tight belly shirt, and it's exposing her pierced little navel, and the jeans that she has on are fitting her body perfectly. Damn, and I had no idea that she has a body like this. Dina is a lot finer than I thought; this girl is actually thick.

She is only thirty years old, so her body is still as tight as a drum. Her brunet hair flows all the way down to her butt, and her smile is as invigorating as a breath of fresh air. Damn, for the first time in months I'm actually moved by someone emotionally, and I'm also physically attracted to her.

Wow, I like this girl already, and I can tell that the feeling is mutual just by the way that she's looking at me. We spend most of the evening talking and getting to know each other while listening to some soft music. Then all of a sudden, she looks over at me and says, "Sergio, you can come a little closer to me. I promise you that I won't bite. At least not on the first date, but I can't predict the future," she says with a seductive smile on her face.

Well, she definitely doesn't have to tell me that twice, so I immediately get closer to her. While I'm trying to finish my conversation with her about my line of work, she slowly leans over toward me and starts passionately kissing me. After the kiss, I take her by her hands and look at her in the eyes and ask her, "What took you so long?" She starts laughing and says, "Sergio, I was just about to ask you the same thing."

Weeks pass and Dina has been spending a lot of time with me. She wants to move in with me, and I have been considering it for the past two days. Today I'm going to tell her yes, and I know that she's going to be happy about that. She has a very good job, so she'll be gone for the better part of each day, and that will give me more than enough time to have my own space.

Not only that, but I must admit that she has made a positive impact on my life. Since I have being seeing her, I have not had the desire to smoke crack. It's amazing how God brings the right person around at the right time for any changes that are to be made in one's life.

Dina and I certainly have a few cultural differences. She likes to do a lot of things outside that I am not comfortable with, one of them being camping; she has been trying to get me to go with her for weeks. I am definitely not going to sleep in the freaking woods, so she can forget about that shit. The only way that's going happen is if I'm in a situation where I have to hide from the police.

Just last week, Dina and I went with a friend to a clear-water park. It's a beautiful park with miles of clear running water that's only knee-deep. On hot, sunny days, people like to walk up and down the park in the water with their shorts on. Most of the females wear bikinis because there are several areas designated for swimming also.

So there I was like a fly in buttermilk, surrounded by nothing but crackers. Dina's friend took along her two young daughters, and all four of them had on bikinis. As I walked along the park in the water with them, I could feel all the attention drawn upon me. Those crackers had huge Confederate flags attached to their airboats and also hanging all over the place.

They were looking at me as if to say "Who in the hell does this nigga think he is?" I was walking around the park with four of the prettiest white females there, and they couldn't stand me for it. I did a good job at keeping my composure and making it seem as if it doesn't bother me, but in all reality, I was very uncomfortable. I couldn't wait to get the hell out of there, so after hanging out for an hour or so, I let it be known.

Today Dina and I are having dinner with my dad and stepmother, and she seems to be very excited about that. My stepmother thinks very highly of Dina, and the both of them get along very well together. Dina helps her in the yard with gardening, landscaping, or anything else that she may possibly need help with. Most beautiful girls have their nose stuck up in the air, but Dina is very down-to-earth.

She will even get up under a car with me to help me work if I asked her to. She's nothing short of being 100 percent behind me, no matter what task is in front of me. My dad tells me all the time how good of a woman he thinks that she is, and he advises me that I should keep her. Not only him, but my stepmother feels the same way. She frequently says to me, "Sergio, now that's the kind of girl that you suppose to marry."

She's absolutely right because Dina is by far the best girlfriend that I've ever had. I trust her, and I have a lot of love for her, but unfortunately I'm not ready to make that kind of commitment. The number one reason being is that I can't put anyone else before my daughter. It's not that I want to get back with Candy, because I could never love her again. It's simply because I don't want to bring another woman in my daughter's life right now.

I only have a couple of months left on my probation here, and I have every intention to go back to Atlanta. One part of me would love to take Dina with me and start a new life with her in the city. The other part of me doesn't think that it would work out, and I haven't a clue as to how my daughter would take it.

However, I do feel obligated to ask her, being that we have been in an exclusive relationship for seven months. I have no idea as to how I'm going to deal with it if she says yes, because I don't expect to hear that. If she says no, then the situation will be easier to handle, because even though she may possibly be the best girlfriend that I have ever had, I'm still not in love with her.

A few days later, the right opportunity presents itself, and I ask her if she wants to move to Atlanta with me. She looks at me as if she's flattered that I asked her, and she says, "No, Sergio, I don't think that would be a good idea." She also says that she doesn't want to be in the middle of my baby mama's drama. I can respect that, and I definitely wouldn't want her to follow me all the way to Atlanta to be unhappy.

Now that I have that issue out of the way, I can start focusing on exactly how I'm going to carry out my plan. Once I get back to Atlanta, I have to find a job and another crib big enough for me and my daughter. No matter where I move, I will always have a room set up for my daughter. I also would like to have a separate room set up just for my musical equipment.

A couple of months later I'm finally free. I finally completed my probation with the state of Florida successfully. I had been spending as much time as possible with Dina for the past two months, knowing that it was inevitable for us to go our separate ways. Now at the last moment, which is today, all of a sudden she changes her mind and wants to go to Atlanta with me.

Damn, this has really caught me off guard, and I was definitely not expecting this. She's crying like a baby, asking me to take her with me. I feel for her, but the car is loaded, my furniture and other possessions are in a storage unit, and I'm ready to hit the road. I refuse to let her change my game plan at the very last minute, knowing very well that I asked her to come with me two months ago.

She has had plenty of time to change her mind within the past two months, but she chose not to, so now it's too late. I have already made plans as to where I'm going to stay, where I'm going to work, and the goals that I would like to accomplish. She cut her own self out of the plan by telling me no two months ago.

Crack 2

Before you know it, I'm back in the ATL, and everything is everything. I have a very extensive background in the automotive industry, so it doesn't take me long at all to find a good-paying job. I have worked for Chevrolet, BMW, Pontiac, Buick, Chrysler, Ford, and Range Rover as an automotive technician. I've also worked for Goodyear, Firestone, and Midas as service manager.

I also have store management skills acquired from being an assistant store manager for AutoZone. Oh yeah, I wouldn't want to leave out all the independent shops that I worked at as well. I have roughly about twenty years of experience in the field along with six ASE certifications, so I guess it would be fair to say that I know my way around cars.

I found a job on Buford Highway that's paying me between eight hundred to 1,100 dollars per week. My friends always wonder how I'm able to rebound so quickly and find good jobs. Well, I can't take the credit for anything because I know that it's the power of God that makes these things happen.

Within four months, I'm moving into a nice house off King Road in Stone Mountain. When I walk out of my front door, I can literally see the mountain from the front yard. The house has four bedrooms, with two and a half bathrooms. It's a fairly large house, considering that I live here all alone, and the neighborhood is very clean and quiet, just the way that I like it.

Out of the blue, I received a telephone call from my oldest son today. He asked me if he could come down from Pittsburg to live with me here in Atlanta until he can find a place here of his own. I told him that as long as I had a roof over my head, he was always welcome to come.

Wow, I haven't seen my son in seven years. He's twenty-three years old now, and the last time that I saw him, he was only sixteen. I was with Mango at the time, and his mother called me and said that she couldn't handle him anymore. He came to live with me here when Mango and I were living in Clarkston.

Damn, I must admit that my son and I don't have a peachy history. He's going to be here tomorrow, so maybe I better bring you up to speed on the situation. When he was four years old, his mother came to Atlanta to make an attempt to get me to marry her. His mother and I had a small argument inside the car, in front of him, and he got mad and called me a black motherfucker.

I looked at him and asked him, "What did you just say?" And he had the balls to repeat it. So when he repeated it, I lightly popped him on his mouth and told him not to ever talk to me like that again. He got so mad that he opened up the backseat car door, got out of the car, and proceeded walking up the street. So there I was chasing behind his little ass to get him back in the car. I knew at that very moment that my son wasn't going to be any joke.

To this day, he still remembers that shit, and from time to time he brings it up. Anyway, at the age of sixteen he came to live with me in Clarkston. His mom had him in private schools all his life, so he's extremely smart. When he first arrived, his mind was on the books and sports, but after being there with me for six months or so, he changed and wanted to be a thug.

My neighbors were telling me stories about him and a few other kids playing with guns. I heard that they would pick up a stray cat and put a nine-millimeter bullet through its head just for the fun of it. One evening when I came in from work, he hadn't done any of his chores. When I confronted him about it, he reached behind himself as if he had a weapon, and I immediately planted him inside my wall.

"Dad, Dad, what's wrong with you?" he screamed. "Why did you rush me like that?" As I grabbed his hand and pulled him out from inside the sheetrock, I looked at him and said, "I thought you were reaching for a gun, son." I immediately apologized to him, but I felt like I had to sleep with one eye open at all times in my own crib at that point. I was no longer comfortable with him there, and I knew that the situation wasn't good for either one of us.

After a couple of weeks pass, he agrees to go back home to his mother's place on the Greyhound. So we said our good-byes and wished each other well. Two days after I see him leave on the bus, Mango and I come home to a big surprise. My neighbor tells me that the police had just taken my son away from the front door.

"My son was here. Are you sure about that?" I asked. "Yes, Sergio," he says, "your son sat on the porch for about an hour before the police finally came and picked him up." Oh shit, I called the police, and he was right; they have my son there, and they won't release him to me either. They said that they would have a hearing in three days with me and the mother to see who was at fault in the situation.

I couldn't believe that shit; his mother sent him back to me without calling me or saying a word about it. Damn, and I was sure that my son felt like neither one of us wanted him. I felt so much guilt in my heart about that scenario, and I still carry that guilt with me now. So I called his mother up and told her that she had to drive all the way here to be in court within three days.

She was so pissed, but it was her own fault because what she did was so stupid. She has six years of college education in psychology, so I would've never imagined her doing something as stupid as that. In court the judge was pissed off at her because she didn't inform me that my son was coming. His final question was who had custody of the kid forty-eight hours prior to being picked up by the police, and that was her.

He released my son back to his mother and told her to take him home. She didn't take him back home with her; instead she let him go down to Florida to stay with his grandmother. By the time Mango and I moved to Florida, my son was into all kinds of criminal shit. Selling dope, doing stickups, assaults, home invasions, you name it.

As a matter of fact, they released him from juvenile into my custody. So there he was again living with me, but that time, everything was cool between us. The last time that I saw him was when I was falsely accused of domestic violence and sexual assault against Mango. He came to the jail to visit me with my dad, and I can still remember him giving me the keep-your-head-up sign.

So all in all I feel like I have failed him, and now he's twenty-three years old. Unfortunately, I can't rewind the clock, so all I can do at this point is try to establish a relationship with him now. Tomorrow he will be here, and we'll just have to see how it goes. I have every reason to believe that everything will be just fine.

The next day, T arrives, and damn, this boy looks just like me. I definitely can't deny him as my son because it's like I'm looking in a freaking mirror. After he gets unpacked and all settled in, he and I make our rounds on visiting the family. I even take him over to Candy's crib to meet his little sister K for the first time.

As soon as he sees her, he says, "Damn, Dad, she is absolutely gorgeous." Then he says, "I don't mean to make it sound like we are some pretty boys or something, but she looks just like us, only she's a girl and she is prettier." I look at him and say, "You got that right, T. She is a pretty little girl." T and K click right from the start, and it's almost as if they've known each other for years.

I would love to take T and K over to meet their other little brother, A, but getting in touch with Peaches to make that happen is easier said than done. I have never seen the three of them in the same room together, and one of these days I would love to see that happen. Since I can't get a hold of Peaches right now, I show T a picture of his little brother, A, and he says, "Dad, he doesn't look like us."

T and K have the same skin tone that I have, but A is light skinned, so maybe that's what he's comparing. I think that A has some of my features, but mostly he looks like his mother, Peaches. I rarely see or talk to him because his mother's side of the family makes me feel like I'm a bad influence on him. They act as if they all are more holy than thou.

I advised T to go out and find a job, because if he plans on staying here, he has to have some type of income coming in. After filling out applications for a month, he's beginning to get frustrated because he hasn't received a single call for a job interview. I know that he's getting stressed out because he is not accustomed to being without money.

I suggested that maybe he should try working for a labor agency that pays daily for odd jobs. He reluctantly agrees and leaves at six o'clock the next morning. When he arrives back at the house, I'm sitting at the table, looking over my monthly bills. He says, "Dad, look at this shit. I've been working all day, and this is what they gave me."

He places the check on the table, and I pick it up to look at the amount. "Damn, it's only thirty-nine dollars." He looks at me and says, "Dad, I can't work all day for that. Shit, I can make that in the streets in ten minutes." I look at him straight in the eyes and say, "Maybe so, son, but you don't have to watch your back when you make honest money."

I tell him to sit down and listen to me, then proceed to advise him to do the right thing. "T, you can't depend on a future of selling drugs and doing crime to take care of a family, because sooner or later that will all come crumbling down. The money might be fast and plentiful, but what's going to happen when you get busted or, even worse, killed?" He says, "You're right, Dad, but right now that's all I know how to do, and I'm good at it."

I respond by saying, "T, you are a grown-ass man now, so I can't make you do anything, but I expect you to do the right thing. If you need training to learn a skill or trade, then I will be more than happy to assist you in achieving that. However, I can't help you if you decide to go out and do something stupid and end up in trouble or dead. I think that you should really put some thought into going back to school and learning a trade."

Damn, that little talk that we had must've gone in one ear and gone out of the other because two days later, I see him bagging up crack cocaine. I guess the little nigga up the street put him on point, because I notice that they have been hanging out a lot lately. I confront him and say, "I guess this means that you're not considering going back to school." He looks at me and says, "I'm sorry, Dad, but I have to do what I have to do."

Now I'm concerned about where he's going to sell the crack, because I'm definitely not going to have any traffic coming to my house. Furthermore, there are no crackheads walking around in this neighborhood anyway. I can't change his mind about selling drugs, so now I have to make sure that he don't get popped because he's on someone else's turf.

I called up one of my partners so that I can purchase a throwaway pistol and a shoulder holster. I know a lot of places where he can sell, but he's going to have to take it over. After checking out different places for him to get his hustle on, he decided to set up at an apartment complex on Candler Road.

He went in there fearlessly, so the guys who were already there instantly gave him his respect. They know that T is strapped and he won't hesitate to pop a cap in somebody's ass, so they let him do his business with no problems. Damn, my son has only been here for a month and he has already taken over the complex.

Two weeks later, T comes to me and asks me if he can bring his girl here from Pittsburg. I agree to it so he catches the bus back up north to go and get her. When he gets back, he has a seven–year-old girl with him, and I say, "Damn, T, I didn't know that you had a daughter. What's her name?" He says, "I don't, Dad, this is my girlfriend's daughter, and her name is D."

I thought when he said that he wanted to bring his girl back, he was talking about a woman, not a child. So I ask him, "Where is D's mother, and when is she coming?" He says, "She'll be here in a week or so, Dad, as soon as she finishes what she got going on up there." I look at him, and then I look at little D and say, "I surely hope so, T."

Wow, now I have a little girl in the house, and I have to make sure that she's taken care of. T is in the streets almost every night, so he can't watch her. I guess he's depending on me to do that for him. It doesn't take long for me to get attached to little D because I love kids, and not only that, but K is not here with me. I have a room full of girl toys and shit for my daughter, K, but unfortunately, Candy won't let me keep her overnight.

Reluctantly, I get little D all set up in K's room. I really don't want to do that, but K is never here to enjoy it herself. Afterward, little D and I hit the stores and I bought her some new clothes and shoes. I also went to the grocery store and bought her all the types of food that she likes. I want to make sure that she's all right, being that her mother is not here yet and I'm working through the day. I don't think that T is quite ready for the responsibility.

Weeks have passed and I still haven't seen the child's mother yet. T keeps on telling me the same thing over and over again; he says that she's coming soon. In the meantime, I have to wash and style little D's hair, cook her dinner, wash and iron her clothes, and keep her company at night while he's in the street, selling crack cocaine. She and I have developed quite a little bond with each other, and I treat her just as if she were my own daughter.

Now when she calls out for me, she calls me Grandpapa Sergio, and every time that I hear her call me that, it melts my heart. Shit, I've been taking care of her for two months now, and I could care less if her mom comes or not. I love her and treat her as if she were my own daughter, and there's nothing that I won't do for her if she asks me.

With me not dating anyone at the present time, little D gets all my attention when I'm not at work. I take her everywhere that I go, and she's just like my little shadow. T also realizes how much I love her, so he gives me complete authority with any matters concerning her. He won't do anything with her without inquiring with me first.

Finally after two and a half months, little D's mother has arrived at the Greyhound station. When we arrive there to pick her up, she's wearing pajamas and slippers. I know that something is not right with this picture, so I look over at T and ask, "What's up with the pajamas, and is that your girl?"

He says, "Yes, Dad, that's her in the pajamas and slippers." As he gets out of the car to help her with the luggage, I notice how skinny she is, and I come to a quick conclusion that she's addicted to crack cocaine. T introduces her to me as Yellow, and after the introduction, we proceed to head back to the crib.

On my way back home, I'm thinking that the reason Yellow took so long to get here is because she's been too busy getting geek. She looks as if she hasn't been asleep in days and hasn't had a meal in weeks. It's a damn shame because underneath the surface, I can see that she really is a beautiful girl.

Once we get back to the house and all the dust settled, I sit the both of them down to go over my house rules. Before I can even finish what I'm saying, Yellow starts screaming at little D about something stupid. "Oh, hell no," I said, "you might as well add these rules to my list. You will not be screaming at little D, and you will not be whipping her under no circumstances in my house."

Yellow then looks over at T as if he were supposed to override what I just said. He looks at her and says, "My dad has been taking care of little D ever since she came here, and he's quite fond of her, so he definitely means what he said." I realize at that very moment that little D has been going through some serious verbal abuse and, quite possibly, physical abuse also. The way that Yellow just snapped and screamed at her is definitely something that she's been doing for quite some time.

School started in my area two weeks ago, so the next day, I advise Yellow to register little D in school. She wants to procrastinate longer and just sit on her ass all day, but I'm not trying to hear that, so I take them to the school anyway. Reluctantly, she drags her ass up to the school administration office and eventually gets little D registered.

While we are out and about, she asks me to take her to the Department of Family and Children Services so that she can apply for some assistance for her daughter, little D. She's quite pissed off about it and has no problem discussing her and T's business with me. She says, "I can't believe your son. He had me to come all the way down here and he don't have shit. He don't have a job, he don't have a car or his own place to stay, so what the hell did he tell me to come here for?" she says.

She's complaining so much that it's starting to get on my nerves and irritate me to the point of telling her to shut the hell up. When we finally get back to the house, she immediately starts on T; she's criticizing him right in front of me for not having his shit together. He's starting to get really pissed off about it, so I advise the both of them to just chill out.

As I turn and start walking out of the room, I hear a sudden slap followed by a loud scream. When I turn around, Yellow is standing there, holding her face, crying, and T is just standing there looking stupid. "What in the hell did you hit her for?" I ask. "Have you lost your freaking mind?"

I sit him down and have a man-to-man talk with him and explain to him that it's terribly wrong for him to hit a woman. He's lucky that she doesn't call the police, because if she does, he will definitely be going to jail. Her eye is already swollen and turning purple, and it looks pretty damn bad. I am so upset with this nigga right now because I can't believe that he thought it would be all right for him to even do some shit like that around me.

Days later, Yellow asks me to take her to a couple of stores, and everywhere that we go, people look at me thinking that I'm her husband and that I physically abused her. It's a very uncomfortable feeling, but I can understand their perception of the matter. She does look as if she's been extremely abused, and it looks as if someone beat the hell out of her.

As the weeks pass, T has been serving her crack to keep her quiet. She's still a time bomb waiting to explode as far as I'm concerned, so I keep an eye out on the both of them. She's still complaining to T constantly about money every day, and I know that he's under a lot of pressure from her. Even though he makes money hustling, it is obviously not enough for her or what she's accustomed to, because she constantly rides his ass every day.

Two months go by and it's basically the same shit going on; my quiet and peaceful little house has been invaded by confusion and the spirit of the devil. When I was here all alone, there was a good spirit in the house, but now it doesn't feel the same because of all the arguments and stress that's going on.

I just got home from work, and I'm in the backyard, smoking a blunt, and playing with T's two pit bull puppies. When one of the pups runs to the side of the house, I immediately run to catch it before it gets into the front yard. As I rise with the puppy in my arms, I notice that there are two unmarked police vehicles parked in the street in the front of my house. Oh shit, what are they doing here, and whom are they looking for? I wonder.

When I enter the house through the back patio door, standing in my living room are two investigators talking to Yellow. "Can I help you, gentlemen?" I ask. "What in the hell is going on?"

"Are you Mr. Lovett," they ask. "And do you have a son named Black?"

"Yes, I am Mr. Lovett," I reply. "Would you like to identify yourselves?" I ask. "Yes, of course," he replies. "I am Special Agent Williams from the FBI, and this is Detective Dupree from the Atlanta Police Department."

"Well, what brings you gentlemen here?" I ask. "Because this happens to be Stone Mountain." He looks at me straight in the eyes with a cold facial expression on his face and says, "Mr. Lovett, we are investigating a bank robbery that happened in the downtown area, and we have reason to believe that your son was involved."

"Are you freaking kidding me?" I ask. "You actually think that my son was involved with a bank robbery."

He says, "Mr. Lovett, whoever robbed the bank dropped a business card onto the floor out of their pocket by mistake." The name on the card happens to be Yellow, and it has her phone number and address in Pittsburg on it. He then says that he called the number and spoke with Yellow's mother, and she informed him that Yellow was here in Atlanta. After researching the computer, he found that Yellow had used my address for several different purposes.

After putting all the evidence and facts into play, he says that everything is pointing at my son, and he wants to talk to him. While he's talking to me, I notice that the other detective is walking around, picking up different items and placing them back down. He's pretending that he's casually looking at my decor, but in all actuality, he's planting a freaking bug somewhere.

Damn, this is some serious shit. I got the freaking FBI in my house, looking for my son. It's a good thing that he's not here right now because I don't have a clue as to what's going on with him. Finally, after questioning me for ten minutes, they decide to leave. As he passes me his business card while he's on the way out, he pauses and looks at me in the eyes and says, "I'm sure that I'll be wrapping this one up pretty quick, Mr. Lovett."

Ooh shit, man, this has got to be a freaking bad dream. My house and cell phone are bugged, and for sure I'll be followed and watched now for who knows how long. I can't wait until he gets his little ass here so that I can find out what's really going on with him. This is the kind of shit that you see on television. I'll have to talk with him outside the house because the inside of the house has been bugged.

Two hours later, T finally pulls up in the driveway, and I go outside to meet him before he gets to the front door. As soon as he sees me, he knows that something is wrong, just from looking at the expression on my face. I lead him to the backyard and say, "T, the freaking FBI just left here two hours ago looking for you. They said that they have reason to believe that you were involved in a bank robbery, and he left a business card for you to get in touch with him."

As I slowly pass him the business card, our eyes lock into each other, and at that point he doesn't have to say a word because I know what the deal is. I inform him that the house is bugged so that he doesn't say anything incriminating once he goes inside to talk to Yellow. Damn, this is a very unfortunate situation, and I know that my son has to leave here now. The last thing that I need is for the SWAT team to come and bust down my freaking door in the middle of the night, looking for him.

Thirty minutes later, I'm dropping T off at a safe destination, where he can chill until he's ready to get somewhere. When I get back to the crib, I immediately advise Yellow that I will be moving out of the house soon. There is no way that I can live here comfortably again, knowing that there are bugs in the house.

Two days later while I'm in the backyard, feeding the puppies, my neighbor calls me over to the fence and asks, "Is everything all right?" I tell him yes, but then he asks me if I am sure about that. So I ask him, "Do you have something that you want to tell me?" He looks me in the eyes and says, "Yes, Sergio, there is something that I need to ask you about."

"The FBI came over to my house a couple of days ago," he says. "And they wanted me and my wife to tell them about anything that we may have seen suspicious going on over at your place. They even offered us a thousand dollars for any information that we may have, and shit, Sergio, you know that Christmas is just around the corner, so that money sounded pretty good."

"What's going on over there?" he asks me. "The feds don't investigate no bullshit, so it must be something serious. The only time that you're going to see the feds involved is when there's a murder or bank robbery," he says. I look at him and say, "Hey, man, they think that my son has something to do with a freaking bank robbery, but I think they've made a big mistake on his identity."

"Ooh shit," he says, with a look of astonishment on his face. "That's some serious shit, Sergio. I hope that everything comes out all right."

"Yeah, it is serious," I reply. "But I'm sure that everything will be just fine." The very next morning, as I'm getting into the car to go to work, another one my neighbors stops me and tells me the same thing. He said that the FBI offered him a thousand dollars for any information that may be consanguineous to his investigation.

Damn, now I know that I have to move from the house soon, being that all my neighbors have been questioned about me and my son. I feel very uncomfortable now, and someone is already following me as I drive to work this morning. This is going to be a trip being trailed by the feds everywhere I go, and I'm starting to get a little paranoid already even though I didn't do shit.

A couple of days later, Yellow and little D are gone, and I'm almost ready to vacate the premises also. I have just about everything packed already, so I'll be out of here in a couple of days or so. Tonight while I'm here all alone for the first time in months, I'm going to pick up this little trick around the corner and get my freak on.

I've been seeing this particular girl hanging out around the corner for weeks; she's cute and fine as can be. I can tell that she's fresh in the game of smoking crack because she doesn't appear to be physically affected by it yet. I'm under a lot of stress, so maybe this will take my mind off things for a while tonight. I'm also a little reluctant to go to my dope boy's house because I haven't been there in quite some time, not to mention that I'm being followed by the feds.

Damn, I got the girl and the dope, and I made it back in the house safely with no problems. I'm sure that the feds know what's up, so maybe after they see this, they'll stop freaking following me around. I'm going to give this trick the first blast of crack so that she can get hot and take her clothes off. The heater is already on ninety degrees, so it shouldn't take her long at all.

Five minutes later, she says that she's hot, and she immediately starts taking her clothes off. Damn, this girl has a very nice body, and she's pretty as well. As I look at her body, I'm inhaling the smoke from the crack pipe simultaneously, and it's a rush within itself. After sitting there looking at her naked body momentarily, my attention immediately shifts and starts focusing on the front door. Ooh shit, man, I'm paranoid now, and the feds are going to bust my door down at any moment.

The crack has me so high and paranoid that I have no interest in the girl whatsoever. Instead of me getting my freak on, I spend the entire night smoking and watching the front door. I'm so paranoid that I make the girl walk back to wherever she has to go, because I am definitely not leaving the house for anything tonight.

Finally, after I trip for most of the night thinking that the police was going to bust through my door, daylight comes and I couldn't be more relieved. I'm still a little under the influence of the drugs from last night, but today I have to finish getting my shit packed so that I can get out of here.

I got so high last night that the puppies wouldn't even come to me. They say that animals can see spirits, and I truly believe that, because before I started smoking the crack last night, they had no problem with playing with me. As soon as I got high, they wouldn't have anything to do with me. They literally ran and hid from me as if I had the spirit of the devil inside me.

A couple of days later, I'm out of the house and staying at an extended-stay hotel on the other side of town. The feds are still following me around, and I'm starting to get seriously annoyed by the ordeal. When I got off work today, I went back to the hotel to take a shower before taking them on a ride in some of the roughest neighborhoods in the city. After riding for two hours all over the city, I picked up another fine-ass trick and headed back to the hotel for a night of fun.

Damn, as soon as I hit the crack pipe, the paranoia started to set in. Here I am staring at the freaking door again, anticipating the police busting through it at any given moment. If they have evidence showing that my son may be possibly involved with a bank robbery, then I'm sure that they may feel I was involved as well.

Weeks pass, and I've been ripping and running all over town every night, picking up tricks for entertainment. Shit, you would be surprised at the people who smoke crack undercover. There are some beautiful girls caught up in the game, and I know where to find them and how to exploit them.

It seems as if the devil has taken over my spirit, because as long as I'm smoking crack, he no longer attacks me in my dreams. I guess he thinks that he has me now, and I'm at a point of no return. He's wrong about that because I still belong to God, and God still loves me. Some people would say that I'm a hypocrite to talk about God while I'm high. I don't agree with that because the Bible says, "In all your ways acknowledge him."

I pray every night even though I'm high on crack cocaine. I know that God doesn't like what I'm doing, but he still loves me anyway. Men put levels on sins; he says that one is worse than the other, but to God, a sin is a sin. Even though I'm far off course to the road leading to God, I know that he has his angels watching over me. I could've been robbed or killed many times by now, but there's a hedge of protection around me, and I know it.

Months pass and I have been all over the place, smoking crack. I stay at one hotel for a week, and then I move into another one the following week. I've been uptown, downtown, midtown, and all around doing my dirt. I know that sooner or later, God is going to put a stop to this idiocy; it's just that I don't know when and how.

I'm what you would call a functional crack addict because I still have a great job, transportation, and a roof over my head. I work six days out of the week, and I'm never high during the day. I only get high at night because I'm embarrassed about what I'm doing, and I wouldn't want any of my customers to see me all pixilated on drugs.

Today is payday, and I usually buy an eight-ball of crack to carry me through the weekend. I don't like going back and forth to the trap to buy more once I start getting high, so I make sure that I have enough beer, cigarettes, and whatever else I desire before I even get started. I already know that as soon as I smoke that shit, I'm going to be paranoid and scared to come back out.

Damn, I have an eight-ball of crack cocaine in my pocket and I'm backing out of the driveway of my supplier's house. I see a police officer coming down the street, and he literally stops his car as I'm backing up. He patiently waits for me to get in the street so that he can get behind me. Ooh shit, man, this is it. The inevitable is about to happen. My spirit has been dead again for quite some time, and God is tired of my crap, so I already know that the policeman is going to arrest me.

The officer pulls up behind me and turns on the blues, but before I stop my car, I stash the crack underneath the carpet. Once he runs my name through the system, he finds out that I have a warrant out for my arrest for child support. He never even questions me about drugs, alcohol, or weapons. Actually, he only stopped me because of the drive-out tag on the car.

Before you know it, I'm dressed out in orange jail clothes, carrying a worn-out mattress to my cell. As soon as I walk in the pod with the other inmates, someone says, "We got some fresh meat today." I stop in my tracks and drop the mattress on the floor, then I grab my dick and say, "Yeah, nigga, I got your fresh meat right here, so come on and get it."

The entire pod got silent for a moment as I look around for the guy that opened his big mouth. I then proceed to my cell upstairs to get my shit situated. A Mexican guy is the houseman, so he comes to my cell and introduces himself. When he asks me for my name, I look at him like he's crazy and tell him to get out of my face.

I'm not surprised that I'm here, but still that doesn't make me happy about it. I'm as mean as a rattlesnake, and everybody knows that it'll kill you, so they all keep their distance. I don't look at anyone and I don't talk to anyone, so they're trying to figure me out. I heard one guy tell another dude to look at the tattoo on my right forearm, and then he says, "That nigga is an old gangsta, so we better not mess with him."

After three days, I finally loosen up and start talking to a couple of guys. I've been sitting back observing the personalities of everyone, so most of them, I don't want anything to do with them. I only talk to the guys that are involved in the study of the Bible. They have invited me to join them in their studies, and I quickly accepted.

God has me right where he wants me, and now I have no choice but to listen to him. An inmate was released yesterday, and before he left, he gave me his Holy Bible. He looked at me in the eyes and said, "Hey, man, I'm going to leave you my sword, so make sure that you use it to fight off these devils in here."

Fortunately, I don't have a cell mate as of yet, but I know one is coming soon. The pod has thirty rooms, fifteen downstairs and fifteen upstairs. I'm the only inmate in the pod that does not have a cellmate yet. I'm sure that you've heard the old saying, "The Lord works in mysterious ways." Well, I guess this is his way of getting my undivided attention.

The pod only has two showers, so it's always a waiting game to get cleaned up. As I wait for the guy before me to finish in the shower, I notice that he's getting himself extremely excited. He's making funny noises and funny faces while moving around awkwardly. Damn, you've got to be freaking kidding me. This nigga is masturbating.

Ooh shit, man, that is disgusting. Who does that? This fool should do that in his cell alone, instead of contaminating the freaking shower. Now I'm really pissed off, so I tell him to get his nasty ass out of the shower and to clean it up. He refuses, and the next thing you know, I'm all over him, beating his ass from one end to the other.

The correction officers quickly rush into the pod, not to break up a fight, because there is no fight; it's simply just to get me off his ass. Once they find out why I jumped on him, they feel that my assault was commendable, and they make jokes about it. They also remove the guy from the pod and place him elsewhere because they know that there's going to be bad blood between the both of us.

The next day, most of the inmates in the pod want me to take over the houseman position. The Mexican is not too happy about it because the houseman gets a few privileges here and there. The houseman gets to stay out an hour later at night, he gets extra food trays, and he also settles all disputes within the pod among inmates.

They decide to take a vote on the position, and out of fifty-nine guys in the pod, I got forty-eight votes. They clearly want me to run the show, and I have no problem with being the leader because that's who I am anyway. Afterward, I immediately start making changes in the way that they do things, and they all like my ideas.

The food is terrible here, and they only give you just enough to keep you alive. If you don't have money on your books to buy commissary items, then you're definitely going to be hungry at night. I notice that my stool has changed colors recently; it's as black as tar. I'm wondering if it's the food, or do I have some other type of problem? There are times when I really don't feel well.

Two weeks later while I'm in my cell alone, I start feeling very sick. I get so hot that I literally remove all my clothes and lie down on the cold floor to cool my body down. I even have my nose at the bottom of the door so that I can get some fresh air to breathe. Damn, this is not good, and I have never felt like this before.

It's getting harder for me to breathe, and my body is running with sweat even though I'm naked. I've been ringing the emergency buzzer in my cell for the past twenty minutes, and no one is answering me at this point. I'm starting to panic, and now I'm actually getting a little scared because I can barely breathe.

Finally, after thirty minutes of me ringing the door buzzer, an officer opens up the door to my cell. When he sees me on the floor naked and my body is soaked and wet from my own sweat, he says, "Ooh shit, man." He immediately gets on his radio and calls for help, and within seconds four officers are carrying me downstairs to the doctor.

Before they get me out of the pod, I can hear the other inmates asking the officers if I am dead. At this point I'm nonresponsive and completely out of it; my eyes are closed, but I can still hear everything that's going on around me. Once they get me downstairs to the doctor, things take a turn for the worse. I can hear the nurse as she says, "Damn, he has no blood pressure and he's turning white."

The doctor says, "Damn, I can't let this guy die on my watch, so somebody call for an ambulance. We have to get him to Grady Hospital immediately." At that very moment as my life is drifting away, I can see a godly image standing right before me. It's like a bright light radiating from a center point. Shortly afterward I pass completely out, and when I finally awaken, I'm at the hospital, handcuffed to a bed, with tubes and wires attached all over me.

There's a correction officer standing next to the bed, and he says, "Damn, Sergio, we thought that you were going to leave us. How do you feel?" Even though I'm extremely weak and exhausted, I slowly turn to him and say, "I feel like I've been born again." He looks at me and smiles as he says, "I bet you do, man, because you were literally dead."

The doctor comes in shortly afterward and explains to me what the problem was. He says that I had lost four units of blood internally and that they had to do a blood transfusion. He also says that I'm a very lucky guy because I almost didn't make it. Apparently, the black stool that I had been seeing for the past two weeks was blood. He informs me that I will be staying there and they will do more testing.

After spending five days in the hospital, unfortunately, I have to go back to the jail. As I walk back into the pod, the inmates are looking at me as if they see a ghost. I ask them why are they looking at me so strangely, and they all reply, "We thought that you were dead, Sergio." I look at all of them with a smile on my face and say, "I was dead, but God allowed me to come back."

One of the inmates quickly turns to me and says, "Man, you have cheated death, so from now on I'm going to call you Ghost." Damn, I wish that he hadn't said that because that's what everyone is going to call me now. "Hey, Ghost, come over here," one of them says. "I know that you want to join us in Bible study tonight, being that God has spared your life." With tears in my eyes from the statement that he just made, I look at him and say, "Man, I wouldn't miss it for the world."

Later that night, not only do I join them for the study, but I also ask them if I can lead it. Without a second thought, they all agree and tell me to go right ahead. I decide to do the study on death, and I start with Jesus raising the widow's son in the city of Nain. The story can be found in the book of St. Luke, chapter 7, verses 11 through 17.

From there I proceeded to the story of about the death of Lazarus and how Jesus brought him back to life. You can find that story in the book of St. John, chapter 11, verses 1 through 44. The study group started out with only seven guys sitting at the table, but now there are twenty-three guys gathered around the table, listening to me. After telling the story about Lazarus, I end the study with the death and resurrection of Jesus Christ. You can find that story in the book of St. John, chapters 19 through 20.

Wow, the power of Jesus is amazing, and I'm sure that everyone gathered around this table agrees with that fact. After the study was over, a couple of guys pulled me to the side and asked me to lead the class from now on. They said that they enjoyed the way that I taught them about the stories and feel that I have a special gift. I accepted the challenge and told them that I would be honored to teach them what I know.

This means that I'm going to have to study to show myself approved because I definitely don't want to teach them anything wrong. While they play cards, make phone calls, watch television, and fool around all day, I'll be studying the Word. So by the time that Bible study comes around, I'll be on top of things and raring to go.

I've been in this jail for forty-five days now, and finally my court date has arrived. The case is not about Candy and my daughter; instead it's about Peaches and my son. When Peaches initially filed for child support, I was employed at BMW as an auto technician, and I was making 875 dollars per week. According to the previous court order, I was obligated to pay eight hundred dollars per month.

Even though I owe her 4,800 dollars, it's really not that bad if you consider how old my son is. In all actuality, it only adds up to six months of payments. However, I don't work for BMW anymore and I don't make that much money now. When I did try to get the payments reduced, I was told that it would take six months in order for me to get a hearing concerning the matter.

When I get inside the courtroom, Peaches and her representative are looking at a picture of me dressed in a fine Italian suit. They're going to use it to show the judge that I have exquisite taste, in malevolence of me not taking care of my son. Damn, they must think that I have plenty of money, and that couldn't be any further from the truth. Granted, I must admit that I did cut her off because of the fact that she would never bring my son to see me.

There is no bond set for my release, and the only way that I can get out of jail is to purge myself out. The last time that I checked, the purge amount was set at 4,800 dollars. As I am standing in front of the judge, she says, "Mr. Lovett, if you have twenty-four hundred dollars, I can release you today." I look at her and reply, "No, Your Honor, I do not have twenty-four hundred dollars." So she says, "Well, you're going back to jail, next case."

Damn, that was quick; she didn't give me a chance to explain or anything. So they chain me up to the rest of the inmates and load all of us back up on the bus. On the way back, it's bittersweet because some guys are being released today and some are not. The ones that are going home later are talking shit about what they're going to do when they hit the streets tonight. On the other hand, some of the other guys are really pissed off because they're not being released.

Once I get back to the cell, I start studying my Bible again; it's the only thing that keeps me grounded. Some of the inmates call me Ghost, and some of them call me Reverend. I guess they call me that because I'm never caught without my sword in hand. If you see me, then you see it. I get a lot of respect from mostly everyone that's inside this pod, and I also keep down a lot of confusion and fights among the guys in here.

There's this one particular guy that has been saying that the inmates should not listen to me because I am not a real minister of God. He's absolutely right about me not being a real minister of God because I haven't been formally trained or educated in that area. However, he's wrong about they should not listen to me. I have never claimed to be a minister, reverend, bishop, preacher, evangelist, or any of the other terminology he would like to use.

Consequently I invited him to come and join us in the study tonight. Perhaps he will get a better understanding of what's really going on. I'm a sinner just like he is, and I violated the law just as well, but that doesn't mean that God can't use me to deliver a message or spread the gospel. When he comes to the study tonight, I'll have the scriptures to prove that point.

I always have a title for the studies that I lead, and tonight it's called "Do You Really Know Who's Talking to You?" God can use whomever or whatever he wants to get his message across, so it's best to pay attention when someone is talking to you. Even the devil used a serpent to communicate with Eve in the very beginning. You can find that scripture in the book of Genesis chapter 3, verses 1 through 5.

Then I use the scripture about God speaking to Moses from a burning bush. You can find that in the book of Exodus, chapters 3 through 4. Last but not the least, my favorite example is when God used a donkey to talk to Balaam. The donkey said to Balaam, "What have I done to you that you have struck me these three times?" Wow, now that's pretty deep to have a donkey speaking to you. You can find that scripture in the book of Numbers, chapter 22, verses 22 through 35.

When I finally finished with the Bible study, the same guy that said no one should be listening to me apologized. I told him that it was all good and that he didn't owe me any apology. My main concern is merely him getting the Word. I feel like I've been born again even though I'm incarcerated, and I have taken back my spirit from the devil.

Forty-five days later my court date comes around again, and maybe the judge will let me out of here today. I've seen quite a few people come and go since I've been here, and their charges were a lot more serious than mine. I'm in here for child support, and I have no idea as to how long they're going to keep me here.

The process of going to court is very hectic because the guards wake us up at four o'clock in the morning. They round us all up like cattle and give us a lousy breakfast in a holding cell. It's approximately one hundred cases every day, Monday through Friday, so they have four holding cells with twenty-five guys crammed in each one.

After feeding us like cattle and giving certain inmates their medications, they chain us all up together and load us on the bus. We then leave the jail on Memorial Drive and proceed to the courthouse in downtown Decatur. Once we get to the special parking lot, they unload us off the bus and lead us through an underground tunnel to the courthouse. Standing inside the tunnel are twenty armed officers waiting to pat us down.

Not only do they pat us down, but they also look in our mouths and make us remove our socks. Once we are cleared there, we enter the building and proceed to another holding cell. In that cell we wait for God knows how long until our case comes up. While we wait, we always have a group prayer for everyone to have a good outcome on their case.

The officers are extremely repulsive during this process, and I can't stand their asses. Inside the tunnel they have real live ammo to take you out if necessary, but inside the building they use stun guns. They will pull that stun gun out on you at the drop of a hat, and it's as if they're itching to use it.

Once I finally get in front of the judge, she says, "Mr. Lovett, you were here forty-five days ago and I cut your purge from forty-eight hundred dollars to twenty-four hundred dollars. Today I'm decreasing that amount to twelve hundred dollars. Do you have that, sir?"

"No, Your Honor, I do not have twelve hundred dollars," I reply. She says, "You're going back to jail, Mr. Lovett, next case."

Oh well, it is what it is, and I am not going to get myself all stressed out over it, so just take me back to my cell so that I can arm myself with my sword. I have been locked up for ninety days, and that seems like nothing when I'm sitting next to a guy that just got sentenced to five years. Besides that, I didn't kill anyone, so they are going to have to release me eventually.

Once I get back inside the pod, some of the older inmates complain to me about a much younger inmate beating on the door like a drum every night. I have asked him to stop the noise twice, to no avail, so today I'm going to show him how serious I am. He always waits until everyone is asleep to start his little rap show.

The pod has a very high ceiling, so the sound carries all over the place. I have no problem with rap music; actually, I like it, but there's a time and a place for everything. When he's banging on the door, it sounds just like an 808 drum machine going *boom!* The only reason that I have sustained my tolerance this long is because that he looks just like Candy's youngest son.

There are only two sounds that really annoy me in here; he's one, and the other is the sound of the doors unlocking electronically. Can you imagine hearing thirty doors unlock, one after the other, five times within a day? It really gets on my nerves. I am on the fifth floor, and I can even hear the doors unlock on the fourth floor and the sixth floor.

Click, click, click. The doors are open, and I immediately go straight to the young guy's cell that's been banging on the door. This guy is at least six feet five inches tall, and he weighs about two hundred pounds. I grab him by his throat and tell him that if he doesn't stop, I'm going to have to hurt him. A couple of guys grab a hold of me and say, "Come on, Ghost, let him go. He can't breathe."

Damn, now I feel ashamed of myself because I've been walking around with the Bible in my hand, teaching the Word, yet I just lost control of myself. On the other hand, I'm the houseman, so I had to put a stop to his nonsense. There are fifty-nine men inside this pod, and I'm the guy they voted for to keep things running smoothly. I can't show any sign of weakness, so I had to do what I had to do.

My cell is on the fifth floor, and it's on the back side of the jail. Sometimes I just sit up on the top bunk and stare out of the window, and as I do so, I'm amazed at how many people come into this jail. From where I'm sitting, I can see every police officer or detective's car when they bring in a new inmate, and it's very frequent.

Time moves on, and sixty days later I'm headed back to court once again, and I have the same female judge that I've had on the two previous dates. She's been pretty tough on this child support issue, so this time I'm going to tell her a thing or two before she sends me back to jail. I've been locked up for 150 days. Shit, it's about time for her to let me out of here.

Once I get in front of her, she asks, "Mr. Lovett, do you have twelve hundred dollars to get yourself released today?" As before, I reply, "No, Your Honor," but before she says "Go back to jail," I ask her if I can speak with her. She says, "Go ahead, Mr. Lovett, but make it quick." I slowly look at her straight in her eyes and say, "Your Honor, I have served one hundred and fifty days. Unfortunately, I'm not making any money by being there, I'm actually losing money."

"The only beneficiary in this situation is the jail that's housing me, because the state is paying them one hundred and sixty dollars per day for me to be there. My son is not getting one dime of that money, and my child support bill is constantly accumulating. Why waste the tax payer's money for my incarceration, when you have the authority to let me out so that I can go back to work?"

She looks at me with this surprised look all over her face and says, "All right, Mr. Lovett, give me the phone number of your former employer so that I can call and verify that he will give you your job back." So I give her the phone number and name of my former employer without any hesitation, and she immediately walks back into her chambers.

When she returns, she looks at me with a smile on her face and says, "All right, Mr. Lovett, I'm going to release you today. Your former employer said that he would pay you seven hundred and fifty dollars per week if I let you out of here." She says, "So today is your day. Once you get back to the jail, your release is effective immediately."

"Thank you, Jesus, and you too, Your Honor," I reply as I turn to walk away. Finally I'm going home. Well, let me rephrase that because I don't have a home, but at least I'll be free of bondage. I can get another home, so I'm not even worried about that. Actually, I'm not worried about anything because I know that Jesus has my back.

As soon as I stepped back into the pod, the guys started cheering for me; they know that I'm being released today just by looking at the glow that's on my face. They're happy for me because they all know how long that I've been here, for none of them have been here longer than I have. They're also thankful for the teachings of the Bible that I shared with them, and I think that I've contributed to some of them turning toward God.

I know that this may sound crazy, but there's actually a part of me that doesn't want to leave. It's definitely the teaching part because that's exactly what I'm going to miss. Teaching on the outside within a church wouldn't be quite the same, for most of the people there would already feel that they are more holy than thou.

I have really enjoyed this experience and time with God, and I have so much of the Word in me that when I open my mouth, I know that it's going to come out. I'm anointed and full of the Holy Ghost, and that was shown to me one night here in a study. I'll never forget the night when this white guy who was a skeptic joined us in Bible study one night. He stood right beside me as we were praying, and when he put his hand on my shoulder, the spirit came out of me and jumped right inside of him.

When he touched me, he immediately started crying, dancing, and running around the pod, saying, "Thank you, Jesus! Thank you, Jesus!" over and over again. When he finally settled down, everyone was looking at him like wow, what in the hell just happened? This guy is supposed to be a nonbeliever. He looked at me with tears running down his face and said, "I believe it now, because as soon as I put my hands on you, Ghost, something came inside of me. Oh, glory, hallelujah! Thank you, Jesus," he said.

Man, I will never forget that moment, God used me for the manifestation of his power. As I distribute all my personal belongings and commissary items away, I'm surprised that some of the guys desperately want my cell. While I was here, I drew spiritual murals all over the walls with colored pencils, and it's actually very nice artwork. Even the correction officers used to stop at my door every time that they passed, just to look at the angels that I drew on the walls.

After we all have one more prayer together, finally over the intercom I hear, "Lovett, pack it up." Damn, that's my cue, and it's time for me to leave here. Once I get downstairs and change back into my street clothes, I ask the Lord to give me the strength to stay diligent in his Word. I know that the devil is on the other side of that door, and as soon as I walk out of here, it's going to be spiritual warfare.

The first day out, I make my rounds with visiting family and friends that I haven't seen for five months. When I finally get a chance to wrap my arms around my daughter, I literally have to hold back my tears of joy because she may not understand why I'm crying. She is so beautiful and intelligent, and one of these days I will surely have her and my younger son, who is also beautiful and intelligent, together living with me.

Satan is already trying to lure me right back into drug addiction because some of the guys that I used to buy crack cocaine from are literally trying to give it to me for free. When I was addicted, they wouldn't give it to me for free, but now that I'm clean, they want to get me started again so that they can get me to start spending money with them.

I rebuked them all in the name of Jesus and told Satan to get behind me. I must keep my eyes on the prize if I'm to amount to anything worthy of the Lord, and I know that he has a purpose for my life, which will enable me to help edify the body of Christ. "God, let thy will be done on earth as it is in heaven," I prayed.

A couple of weeks later, I receive a letter from the Federal Bureau of Investigation, and they want me to testify against my eldest son. Apparently, they have finally caught up with him in Pittsburg and have him confined. They must be crazy if they think that I'm going to say something to incriminate my own son; surely that's not going to happen.

Months later, the court date for my son comes around, and I'm at the Federal Building on Spring Street in downtown Atlanta. The same agent that came to the house during the investigation asks me to go into a private chamber so that he can brief me on all the evidence that he has against my son.

He starts out with all the juvenile charges that I already know about, and then he proceeds to the adult charges. He says that my son allegedly was involved in snatching a purse from a lady at a grocery store parking lot. When the store manager came out to assist the victim, my son allegedly fired several shots at him and ran him back inside the store.

Then he tells me that my son allegedly shot a drug dealer and took his dope. He didn't kill the guy, but he shot him in the leg. From there he goes on to tell me about my son allegedly being involved in a home invasion, and during that scenario, he took the guy's Rolex watch and money.

I thought that he was finished at that point, but then he proceeded to tell me about several bank robberies. He says that my son robbed a couple of banks up north and dropped the latex gloves that he was wearing outside the bank. He asks me what I think was inside the gloves, and I respond by saying "DNA."

He then tells me that when my son allegedly ran outside the bank in Atlanta, his baseball cap fell off his head. So he asks, "What do you think was inside of the cap, Mr. Lovett?" And once again I respond by saying "DNA." He says, "Mr. Lovett, you appear to be a very tough guy, and I guess the apple doesn't fall far from the tree because when I asked your son for a DNA sample, he told me to go and screw myself."

"It took five officers to hold him down so that I could swab the inside of his mouth to get the DNA," he says. "It's a perfect match, Mr. Lovett, so I'm trying to get him off the streets for thirteen years because your son is a very dangerous guy. The only thing that I need from you is to say that he was living with you in Stone Mountain at the time that I came to your house," he says.

After the briefing, I went back into the hallway to await the start of the trial. While waiting outside the courtroom, I decided to take a peek inside the window. As I look inside, I can see my son sitting at the defendant's table with his attorney. Damn, he's probably twenty pounds heavier than the last time I saw him, and he doesn't even know that I'm standing behind this door, looking at him.

While I'm sitting there waiting for the case to start, the prosecutor walks up and says, "You can go home, Mr. Lovett, because we don't need your testimony." He says that my son just took the plea bargain before the case started and that the judge sentenced him to seven years. The prosecutor is really pissed off about the outcome because he wanted the judge to give my son at least thirteen years.

As I leave, I'm somewhat relieved to know that my son was only sentenced to seven years, as opposed to thirteen. I say *somewhat* because I don't want to see him sent off to prison at all. When I look at him, I can't see him doing all the things that he's been accused of, and I guess the reason is simply the fact that he's my son.

As time moves on, I'm faced with the fact that both of my younger kids' mothers are doing drugs. At first I couldn't believe it, but after doing a little bit of investigating myself, I found it to be true. The both of them are smoking crack cocaine, and I be damned if I'm going to pay for their drug habits. I can't see anything that they're doing for my kids with the money that I give them, so I'm going to cut the both of them off. From now on, when my kids need something, I'll go to the store and buy it myself.

Peaches gets two hundred dollars from my paycheck every week, and Candy is extremely jealous of that fact, so she has filed for child support also. I also have a case open concerning arrears owed for my eldest son, who's in prison. I'm very much overwhelmed with these child support issues, and I feel like I'm between a rock and a hard place.

Candy should've never taken me to court for child support because I was willingly taking good care of my daughter. However, she's so jealous about what Peaches is getting, so she did it anyway. The courts actually ordered me to pay her less than what I was already giving her, so now she's extremely pissed off and looking stupid.

I cut Peaches off by changing my job. If they don't know where I work, then they can't make any deduction on my check. I even took it a little further by working for a company that pays me commission under-the-table, so as far as the system is concerned, I'm no longer employed. Hey, a brother has to do what a brother has to do, because I refuse to give her two hundred dollars every week to help her kill herself by smoking crack.

My son lives with Peaches's mother and brother, and I must give them credit for taking good care of him. They love him dearly, and there's nothing that they wouldn't do for him. When I go there to see him, his mother is always in the street somewhere, doing drugs. It's gotten to the point that her own family locks her out of the house at night, and sometimes she has to climb in the window to get back in.

It's still hard for me to believe that she's caught up like that, because the household that she was brought up in is seriously grounded in the Word. All three of her sisters are married to ministers, and her mother and brother are heavy in the church as well. So she has a very strong support group behind her, if only she decides to use it. Whenever I walk inside her mother's house, man, I can feel the essence of the Lord there.

Candy, on the other hand, tries to be slick with her shit, but she's smoking crack too. I'm sure that you've heard of the old saying "How can the teakettle call the pot black?" Well, that's Candy in a nutshell. She's fast and quick to talk about someone else, when in fact she's out there doing the same shit herself. She can't fool me though, because I've been there and done that; hell, I'm a connoisseur on crack cocaine.

I don't know how long that it's going to take, but I do know that the god that I serve is going to give me an explosive blessing. A blessing so huge that it's going to launch me above all my enemies. I'll be the lender, not the borrower, and the head, not the tail. Not if, but when he does, I'm going to have all my kids with me.

All the pain, all the trials, and all the tribulations that I've been going through will not be in vain. What doesn't kill me will only make me stronger, and I'm not ashamed of what I've been through. The Bible says, "And we know that all things work together for good to them that love God, to them who are the called according to his purpose." You can find that scripture in the book of Romans, chapter 8, verse 28.

With that being said, I can't in any way, fashion, or form condemn anyone else for what they are doing. It is not my place to judge anyone, for that responsibility belongs to God. Before I try to remove the spec from someone else's eye, I must first remove the plank from my own eye.

All I can do at this point is intercessional prayer for them and hope that they never lose their identity. Even when I smoked crack, I never lost sight of who I am and what I am to God, which is his child. Just like a parent may not approve of some of the things that their child does, the parent still loves that child. The same goes for our Father, who is in heaven. God may disapprove of our sins, yet his grace, mercy, and love never cease. His love is unconditional.

Months pass, and I've been living like a fugitive running from the law. I've been going from hotel to motel so that neither of my kids' mothers can find me. The both of them want to see me locked up in jail, and they wouldn't think twice about calling the police on me. Since I haven't been paying child support, the state has also suspended my driver's license, and now I have to watch my back while driving.

In the midst of putting myself right back into the same element, I allow myself to get caught up in drugs again. Shit, it's like putting a rat in a cheese factory, because every hotel that I go to has girls and dope readily available. At first I start out a little bit here and a little bit there, but now I'm full bloom.

Imagine that, less than a year ago, a white boy put his hand on my shoulders and he literally got the Holy Ghost. Tonight I'm sitting in a hotel room, sweating bullets, looking at the door, with a crack pipe in my hand. Wow, the devil never stops, and I made a big mistake by putting my sword down. I feel like I'm dead again, and I'm doing all the things that I hate to do.

In the book of Romans, chapter 7, verse 19, it says, "For the good that I will to do, I do not do; but the evil I will not to do, that I practice." I seem to think of that scripture every time that I get high, because in all reality, I hate doing what I'm doing. The following verse says, "Now if I do what I will not to do, it is no longer I who do it, but sin that dwells in me." So I already know that the only way to victory is through Jesus; it's just that the sin in me is keeping me from him.

Years pass and I'm living a double life because at daylight I'm one the most professional and experienced auto technicians that you can possibly find in the area where I work. At night, between eight o'clock and midnight I change. I'm like a freaking vampire, sucking the life out of myself and beautiful girls.

Even though these girls are caught up like me in this dope game, I can feel the spirits of most of them when I'm with them. Most of them are pure of heart and have a special purpose in life, but just like me they're fighting unseen spirits. I just sent a girl across the street to the store to buy a pack of cigarettes, and she has only been gone for two minutes, but now I hear a knock at the door and it's making me paranoid.

Shit, there's no way that she can go there and be back this fast. So I look through the sight glass to see who's at the door. Surprisingly it's her, but when I open the door, it's like, ooh shit, it's the freaking police. Man, and they're six officers deep. They scared the shit out of me because they were hiding around the corner, waiting for the door to open.

They all barge into the room and start asking me questions about the girl and also about drugs. Apparently, she's well-known by the police officers, and they saw her when she came out of my room. After searching the room, they find a glass pipe. They can't find any crack in the room, but they do have the pipe. So they lock the both of us up for loitering for drugs, and I'm wondering how in the hell the police can say that I was loitering when, in fact, I was in my room.

They kept me in jail for thirty days on that charge, and now that I'm released, I'm still in the same situation. I work like a dog all week just to pay for my room and drugs. I still carry myself like a professional at work, but at night it's another world, and it's full of darkness.

After another night of getting high in my hotel room, I finally awake to a sickness that is all too familiar. The last time that I felt this way was when I was near death in jail and they had to transport me to the hospital. This is not good, and I'm here in this hotel room all alone. Instead of calling 911, I decide to call my employer, and he immediately comes to take me to the hospital.

When I get inside the emergency room lobby, I immediately request to see a doctor. The receptionist gets an attitude with me and tells me to fill out the necessary paperwork before I can be seen. It takes everything within me to fill out the paperwork, and I'm fading in and out. When I finally manage to make it back in front of her desk with the paperwork, I pass out right in front of her, and my head slams to the floor.

After I awaken and come back around, the doctor explains to me that I have lost three units of blood, and he recommends a blood transfusion. I totally refuse the transfusion, so they have no choice but to put an extra IV in my other arm and wait for my body to replenish itself. As I lay in the intensive care unit with tubes in my nose and arms and wires hooked all over my upper body, I'm reminded that the devil wants me dead.

After two days of lying here and not being allowed to eat, they put me to sleep and place a camera down my throat to find the source of the bleeding. To no avail could they find the source, so they put me to sleep the next day and put the camera up the other end. They still couldn't find the source of the bleeding, so after a week of being in the hospital, I was finally released.

As the time goes by, I get arrested numerous times for driving with a suspended license, so I decide not to drive anymore at all. Tonight I'm riding with this girl that I get high with periodically, and we're on our way to buy some more crack. This time she's going to pay for it because I've already spent at least a hundred dollars.

We pull up in the driveway of the trap house, and she passes me the money, and it is a hundred-dollar bill that she says is for her light bill. The drug dealer comes to my side of the car and asks me what's up. I look at him as I pass him the money, and I reply, "An eighty pack." He passes me the dope, and while I'm looking at the quantity, *click, click*. Ooh shit, this nigga has a forty-five cocked and loaded, pointing at my face.

"What you trying to do, nigga, rip me off?" he says. "Get that freaking gun out of my face, nigga! What's wrong with you?" I reply. He says, "Man, this freaking one-hundred-dollar bill that you just gave me is counterfeit, so give me my dope, nigga."

"Ooh shit, man, I didn't know," I reply as I pass him the dope. "Hey, man, I've been buying dope from you for years, and we've never had a problem like this, so my bad," I tell him.

As we pull out of the driveway, I look over and say, "Bitch, you almost had me killed." Instead of jumping all over her and blaming her for what just happened, I take a good look at myself. Satan wants me dead, and it's only by the grace of God that I'm still alive. That was closer than a close call. That forty-five was no more than eight inches from my face.

Two weeks later I'm at one of my female friends' crib, getting high on crack cocaine again. We've been smoking for most of the night, and I've probably spent at least two hundred dollars smoking with her. It's three o'clock in the morning, and she wants me to leave because I'm out of crack, but the problem is I didn't drive here; she brought me here.

I'm looking at this girl, like are you freaking serious? "It is twenty-eight degrees outside and it's also raining, and you expect me to leave right now?" I ask. "Yes," she says, "and if you don't, I'm going to call the police." That's all she has to say, and I'm out the door. At this point I'm extremely high, and I'm also paranoid that she may have called the police on me anyway, despite me leaving.

My cell phone is inside her crib, so I can't even call for help right now. It looks like I'm going to have to tough this one out. As I walk around freezing at three o'clock in the morning while getting soaked and wet, I desperately look for a place of refuge. The only place that I can find is underneath some hedges in the fallen leaves.

While I lay there under the hedges, trying to keep from freezing, I began to call on the Lord. I take a good look at myself and where I am and say, "This is ridiculous. I'm literally lying in the dirt." As the tears start to fall down my face, behold, the spirit of the Lord appears, and with him is my grandmother. She slowly walks over to me as she sings "Amazing Grace" and gently places a blanket over me. As the blanket covers my head, the spirit of the Lord and my grandmother slowly disappear into the light.

Finally, when I awake, it is daylight, and I feel like an idiot. I know that this madness has to stop, and it has to stop now. I make preparations to move completely to another area so that the temptation won't be so readily available in my face every day. It's going to take some serious soul-searching for me to get myself back on track with God, but I know he still loves me.

Months pass and I've been doing pretty good lately staying away from crack, but now I have another problem that has finally caught up with me, and it's child support. I received a letter from child support concerning Peaches and my son, and they want me to come to their office to discuss the matter, or else they're going to lock me up.

When I get there, they tell me that I owe arrears to the tune of forty-five thousand dollars and they want the money now. The situation changed immediately when I informed the agent on the case that Peaches was in state prison, doing a five-year sentence for fraud. She verified the information, and afterward, she wiped my debt clean. She said that I no longer owe any monies on that case and that it couldn't be reopened by Peaches.

Wow, whoever said that God doesn't perform miracles anymore was wrong, because that was nothing short of a miracle. When I walked into that building, I owed forty-five thousand dollars, and now I walked out owing zero. That was definitely a mountain in front me, and it was removed just like that. Oh, glory, hallelujah, thank you so much, Jesus.

Months pass and I'm relieved to have some breathing room in order to get myself back together. However, now I have Candy to deal with, and she's the worst as far as I'm concerned. She always comes as a wolf in sheep's clothing, and she would love to see me locked up in jail.

Over the years, even though I didn't pay most of my court-ordered payments, I did always take my daughter shopping whenever she called. Even doing that was risky with Candy because I never knew when she might have me set up. She's the "smile in your face, stab you in the back" type, and I can never trust her again.

I've come to the conclusion that I'm going to have to go back to Florida in order to truly recover. I need to be out from under all this stress and pressure of the police coming to get me or even being in the wrong place at the wrong time. I'm sick and tired of going to jail, and I've been praying for the Lord to keep me out of there. I'm not running from the situation; it's just that I know that God can make a way for me to take care of it, if I get myself aligned with him.

So I leave the hotel and start sleeping inside a Suburban that's parked behind the shop where I work. My car is also here and I have painted it, put new tires on it, and it is road ready, raring to go. Granted that I don't have a tag or insurance on it, when it's time for me to go, you can best believe that I'm going to go.

I've been sleeping inside this truck for two weeks now, and it's been just me and the Lord every night in conversation. I know that something is getting ready to change this situation, because I can just feel it in my spirit. I've been using the shower inside the building before close of business, and at night I'm all alone in the dark inside of the truck.

Two days ago I called my daughter from the shop phone, and I forgot to block out my telephone number. She called me back later that day, so now Candy knows where I work. I agreed to meet them at a clothing store so that I could take my daughter shopping, and I was very pleased to see my baby girl. We had a wonderful time together, and I bought her just about everything that she asked for that day. She left me with bags of new clothes and a hug and a kiss.

The very next day as I'm walking toward the front of the shop, the owner is signaling for me to go back. I'm looking at him, like what's going on and why is he telling me to go back? He's adamant about it, so I go back and wait for him. Five minutes later he comes to the back and tells me that the police just left the building, looking for me.

Damn, it didn't take Candy long at all to send the folks to me. I just took my daughter shopping yesterday, and today she sends the police to lock me up. Actually I knew that she would send them for me, but the time that I spent with my daughter was worth it. I'm just thankful to the Lord that he didn't allow them to get me, and I guess that's my cue for me to get out of here. So in all reality I'm not mad or upset about any of this, because I know that this is part of God's plan.

The Pipe Dream

The very next morning, I put a used-car-dealer tag on the back of my car and hit the highway. I'm heading to my dad's house in Florida so that I can get away from all the stress here in Atlanta. I never thought that I would be saying this when I saw the "Welcome to Florida" sign, but I feel like I've been born again. I usually say that when I'm leaving Florida, not when I'm arriving.

Thank you, Jesus. I'm finally pulling up in the driveway of my dad's house, and I made it here with no problems. My dad lives alone, so he's going to be very happy to have me here, at least for now, that is. It's a fairly good-size home and it's designed with two separate sides, so I'll have plenty of room and privacy while I'm here.

As far as what I'm going to do to keep a flow of income coming in, I have no idea right now. What I do know is that I'm putting it all in the Lord's hand. He'll provide me with everything that I need, and I truly believe that because I have faith in him.

I've been clean for a couple of months now, and getting high is no longer an option for me, so I'm going to make a lot of changes. I'll start with what I watch on television, the type of music that I listen to, the type of people that I associate with, the places where I go, and even what I eat, I'm changing that as well.

I going to put all my energy and focus back on the Lord, and I'm going to have to feed my mind and spirit with the Word consistently every day until I get it right. I have nothing here to really distract me, so it's a perfect time and place for me to really get myself built back up in the Word. This time, I'm going to make it a lifestyle, instead of just having knowledge about it and not living it.

A couple of months have passed, and I've been spending most of my time in Bible studies all through the day and night. When I watch television, I find myself drawn to the church channels now, and I only listen to contemporary gospel when enjoying music on the radio. It feels like I'm changing inside out, because I simply have no desire and tolerance for any of the destructive behavior that used to be within me.

The Lord has put a couple of songs on my heart, and I've been working on them for a few weeks now. Fortunately, I brought all my musical equipment with me from Atlanta, and now I'm beginning to see why. It's because the Lord wants me to play for him in church. Actually, I've known this for quite some time, but I just didn't want to do it. I only wanted to play music for my own, personal reasons.

When I used to compose hip-hop and rhythm and blues tracks, I had to put a lot of thought into it. The tracks that the Lord gives me come as a gift; there is literally minimal effort on my part. I've put together enough material to complete an entire compact disk, and I'm going to release it in the near future.

I have no idea as to where I'll be getting the financial resources to do so; what I do know is that the Lord says that it will come to pass. Faith without works is dead, so I'm composing this project now knowing that the Lord will provide me with what is needed at the appropriate time. I've also been instructed to play these tracks in church to build my confidence. I've never performed alone as a solo artist. I've always had my brothers right there beside me.

Another reason is that I'm not playing the traditional type of songs that one may be accustomed to hearing in church. My music is a little different, and some of the older church members may not like it or approve of it. That's all right with me too because I'm actually not targeting people that are already saved and filled with the Holy Ghost. I'm more interested in the sinners, and that's who I want my music to appeal to. If I can help lead just one of them to God, then I've served a purpose worthwhile.

Not only have I been instructed to complete a musical project, but the Lord has also instructed me to write a book and draw a picture. The book is going to be about spiritual warfare within oneself, and I've started and stopped twice trying to write it.

I first started writing it about five years ago, and I got all the way up to page 170. Then one day, Candy got upset with me, and she took a sledgehammer and demolished the computer. To add insult to injury, she then tossed it in the Dumpster while rain was pouring down. She didn't want me to have any possibility of retrieving what I had already written.

I was extremely hurt because I had put quite a bit of time and energy into writing that much. She knew exactly how much the book meant to me, and she also felt that it may possibly bring me some type of success one day. That's something that she definitely doesn't want to see happen. She would rather see me struggling just to survive.

A couple of years later, my brother Don gave me a laptop computer, and I started writing the book all over again. I made it up to page 230, then that laptop was stolen from me. Damn, it's as if the devil doesn't want me to finish the book because he keeps on trying to discourage me. I guess he doesn't want me to write about the power of God and his love, grace, and mercy.

Since I've been here in Florida, I've been instructed to write the book again, and right now I don't even have a computer. However, I know that my resources will be coming soon because the Lord has clearly shown me a vision of the finished works. The art piece, on the other hand, I've never started, but I can see the works as clear as day. It's an image of a woman that's reflecting struggle yet she has the victory.

I shared these visions with one of my friends, and they said that it was merely just a pipe dream, but I beg to differ. God has given me a clear vision of all three of the projects, and I'm definitely going to see it through. The book will surely have a purpose, just as well as the artwork and music, and maybe this is going to be my way of bringing sheep to the fold; only God knows.

I'm officially on the right side of the track now, because the devil has started attacking me in my dreams again. For me that's a clear confirmation that he's angry with me, and I'm happy about that. He never attacked me when I was on drugs and he had control of my flesh, but now that I have God within me, he comes every night to attack me when I dream.

I hate the graphic, life-threatening dreams that keep me up all through the night, but I welcome them if that's what it takes for me to walk with Jesus. Don't get it twisted. I'm still very much under construction, but I'm definitely nowhere near where I was. However, I do feel that I'm ready for whatever the Lord has in store for me.

When I look back on my life at the successes and failures, I can clearly see why the Lord didn't bless me with huge success early in life. It's simply because that I wasn't ready for it and I wasn't willing to do what he wanted me to do. Now that I've finally given in to him, I know that the possibilities are endless.

Today my dad brought a lady and her four daughters over to the house for a visit. She's only forty years old, and as soon as our eyes met, we both know that there's something there. Her name is Ms. Tangy, and she's so fine that it's pathetic. I'm doing my best right now to keep my distance from her while she's here, but we both are definitely attracted to each other.

We manage to stay away from each other all the way up until the point to it's time for them to leave. Then as she and I load the trunk of the car with clothes, our faces unexpectedly come within inches of each other. Standing here looking into each other's eyes, we slowly lean toward one another and kiss, and the moment is magical.

Wow, we both felt that kiss. It was really something special. I must admit that I hadn't kissed a girl in years, because I haven't been in a relationship since I was with Candy. Sure, I've been with a lot of different females when I was getting high, but I never kissed them. I only paid for services rendered; there were never any feelings involved.

Ms. Tangy asked me to come over to her place tonight, so now I'm standing at her front door, knocking. She greets me with a hug and a kiss as if we've known each other for years. I don't know what it is about this girl, but I like her a lot already.

Ms. Tangy has four daughters, and their names are Alia, aged fifteen; AD, aged twelve; Snoopy, aged ten; and Mirror, aged three. Snoopy warms up to me right away. I mean, there is no hesitation at all with her; it is love at first sight. I don't know if it's because she reminds of my daughter or what, but I'm instantly attached to her as well.

Mirror is just a baby, and she's following me around everywhere that I go. I'm sure that you have heard that babies and animals can sense a good or bad spirit within a person. Well, that's the truth, and this baby knows that I have a good spirit, because she's all over me. Wow, I've only been here for one hour and I'm being showered with love from Ms. Tangy, Snoopy, and Mirror. It's truly an honor for a baby to approach me and to want me to pick her up and hold her.

The other two older girls, Alia and AD, are just checking me out and looking at me as if they think that I'm cute and cool. When Ms. Tangy tells them to do something, they are very reluctant to do it, and it seems to have really pissed her off. Now I'm sitting here in the middle of these two girls about to get their ass whipped, and I can't let that happen.

My sister never did get a whipping when we were coming up as kids, and I have never hit my daughter either. I simply will not tolerate Candy or anyone else, as far as that goes, putting their hands on my baby girl. So when Ms. Tangy grabs the belt to hit her girls, I immediately stand between them and say, "No way." I am not going to sit here and watch her physically beat those girls, and I'm letting her know this off the rip.

She then looks up at me with this look of astonishment all over her face and says, "I'm impressed with you standing up for my girls, Sergio, but they are about to get an ass whipping." I look at her straight in the eyes and say, "Not on my watch, they're not. I'm not accustomed to seeing a little girl get hit, and I'm not about to start seeing it today." After she realizes that I'm totally serious about the physical punishment, she acrimoniously backs off.

My actions must have turned her on or something, because immediately after she sent the kids upstairs for the night, she showers me with her love. We spend the entire night with each other cuddling and talking, and I enjoyed every moment of it. However, it's my first night here, so I don't want the kids to see me still here when they awaken.

I'm still not driving my car because of my suspended license, so at six o'clock in the morning, I'm pedaling a bicycle back to my dad's crib, which is four miles away. On the way back, I run into my cousin Nita heading to work, and as soon as she sees me, she says, "Boy, you just got back in Florida and you're creeping already."

I am creeping, but not because of another man; it's because of Ms. Tangy's kids. The three older girls have the same dad, and he's in prison right now. Mirror's dad lives somewhere not too far from here; however, he has a restraining order against him to stay away from Ms. Tangy.

She seems to get upset just by merely speaking of Mirror's dad, and she has actually told me some terrible things about him. I think the worst thing of all is the fact that she said that she caught him urinating on the baby's bottles while they were in the kitchen sink. Wow, that was pretty deep for me, and I've never heard of anything like that before. Who does that? Is that some type of voodoo ritual or what? In any event, it's sickening.

The guy picks up his daughter every other weekend, and he has to pick her up in the police station's parking lot. At this point I don't know all the details of their failed relationship, but from the information that she has shared with me, I don't like him at all. The first chance that I get to meet him, I'm going to let that fact be known, and he's going to know that I don't like him.

As time progresses, I'm spending more time at Ms. Tangy's place than I do at my dad's crib. The kids love me, and I have fallen in love with each and every one of them as well. I spend a lot of quality time with them, I take them to the park, I help them with their homework, and I also cook and clean for them. Whenever I walk through the door, they all jump up and run to me, competing for my personal attention.

For some reason, Snoopy always seems to win, and the other girls are starting to get a little jealous about it. I can't seem to resist her smile and love for me, and I guess it's because it is so genuine. Ms. Tangy always has to tell Snoopy to back off me and let me have some space, because she's always right under me. Snoopy actually asked me if she could call me Dad, and it brought tears to my eyes to know that she loves me that much.

Today I'm in church getting ready to perform the songs that the Lord has given me, and I must admit that I'm a little bit nervous. I've never performed alone before, and at this point I have butterflies in my stomach. As I approach my keyboard, the congregation is exceptionally silent, not knowing what to expect from me.

I start off with a fast song that I call "But Jesus." It's about when I'm in trouble and in need of help and I can't count on anyone else but Jesus. By the time I finish the first verse and approach the chorus, the congregation is on their feet, feeling it. It's on and popping now. I got this, and the butterflies are all gone.

I look over at the church's pianist, and she has a look of astonishment all over her face. Ironically she was my choir director forty years ago, when I first sung lead on the song "Trouble in My Way." She has been playing piano for the Lord as far back as I can remember, and I'm actually a seed that she had sowed. She's the one that inspired me to sing for the Lord when I was just a youngster.

After I end the first song, I get a standing ovation, and I can tell that I caught them all off guard. Surely they didn't expect my style of music. Now that I have their undivided attention, I'm comfortable and confident as I proceed to my last song, which I call "The Lord Is with Me." I get the same response with the last song as I did with the first, and for me that's my confirmation from God.

After the service, I get numerous compliments on the songs, but I didn't write those songs; the Lord did. So as I drive home with no license, I'm not concerned or afraid of the police stopping me anymore because I know that the Lord is with me. Before I even make it to the house, the Holy Ghost gets all over me, and I'm riding down the street with tears running down my face, speaking in tongues.

I hear you, Lord. Yes, indeed, I do, and I'm going to do as I'm told this time for sure. Later that day as I try to share my experience with Ms. Tangy, I can easily detect a jealous spirit coming from within her. She gets a lot of attention from guys because of her body, and I've even heard females say "Damn, that girl is fine." So she's uncomfortable with the attention shifting toward me. She already knows that almost every girl in her complex would jump at the opportunity to get with me, because they've shown it.

Don't get me wrong because I'm not conceited by any means; however, I am a very attractive guy. Her neighbors flirt with me every chance that they get, and she knows it. I just happen to be extremely disciplined when it comes to fooling around on a woman that I truly care for.

Not only do I care for her, but her daughter Alia told me that she's pregnant. Alia has heard some of the conversations that Ms. Tangy and I have had, and she knows that I don't want any more kids. Reason is that I have three kids of my own right now, and I haven't been an essential part of their lives. So I definitely don't want to put myself in that position again.

A week later, Ms. Tangy tells me that she's pregnant, and I have mixed emotions about the situation. I don't want to father another child and end up not being in that child's life for whatever reason. I have a son in prison, and I have a son and a daughter in Atlanta that I can't see unless I have money. So the Lord knows my pain concerning my kids.

Ms. Tangy is elated about the pregnancy, and there's no way that she would abort the baby even if that's what I wanted. All her girls are excited as well, and they're already thinking of names for the baby. Apparently I'm the last person to know what's going on, because as it turns out all her neighbors know that she's pregnant as well.

After marinating a couple of days on the fact that Ms. Tangy is pregnant, I have no choice but to accept it and be happy about it. Just maybe this is the Lord's will, and I'm getting another chance to raise my own child. A lot of guys that have a wife and kids at home take that privilege for granted, but I, on the other hand, have never been able to acquire that.

As the weeks go by, I'm asked to play at a couple more churches. I ask Ms. Tangy and the kids to accompany me, but she's adamant about not going. She says that she doesn't want me to embarrass her by socializing with the women in church. "Are you freaking kidding me?" I ask. "There's no groupies in church. Besides, I'm doing this for Jesus, not for my own self-recognition."

Alia is only fifteen years old, and she tells her mother that if she really loves me, she would be more supportive of what I'm trying to do. Wow, that hit Ms. Tangy right where it's supposed to, and she reluctantly agrees to come. During my performance, the congregation is up on their feet as before, and so are the kids and Ms. Tangy.

When we get back to her crib later, the kids tell me how much they enjoyed the performance, but Ms. Tangy is reluctant to say something positive. I can sense that she's never going to be truly supportive of my goals, and in my mind she's a hater. I got a news flash for her: the Lord has shown me how to motivate from hate.

It's always hard to get someone who knows you to believe in you. Even Jesus had the same problem; they said, "How can you be the son of God? Aren't you the carpenter's son?" So I don't expect my family and friends to believe in me either, but in time they will see the blessing of God on my life, and I'm sure of that.

As the weeks go by, Ms. Tangy is getting bigger, and she's about to bust out of her clothes. I've been pampering her for weeks on end, and she's gotten to be quite spoiled with me cooking and cleaning for her. I've also been asking her to go to the doctor to get herself checked out, but she continues to procrastinate. I'm beginning to wonder why she won't go, and now my spirit is telling me that something is not right.

I made an attempt to get her equally yoked with me and what I'm trying to do for God, but she has a very small mentality. She says that she doesn't want to be with a man that thinks the way that I do and has the goals that I have. She would rather be with an average Joe, scuffling to survive.

I tried to explain to her that I'm not doing what I'm doing for money and fame. I'm doing it because this is what I've been called to do. If financial prosperity happens to come along with the territory, then it's the Lord's will. I played music in nightclubs with my brothers for years, and I've had my share of women and drugs, so that's not what I'm about.

As I ride my bicycle back to my dad's house, I'm thinking this will never work between us. I'm on a different level than she is, and I can't allow her to hold me back. As I approach the house, *bam!* Ooh my god, a car just hit me from behind and threw me across the hood to the ground.

Ooh my god, the devil just tried to kill me. The car must have been doing at least fifty miles per hour when it hit me. I'm hurt, and I'm also in shock. The driver is a very old lady, and she's hysterical; she probably thought that she killed me. "I didn't see you," she says. "Are you all right, sir?"

"Just take me home," I reply. "I live one block straight ahead."

This lady has scared the crap out of me, and I just want to go home. She puts my twisted-up bicycle in her trunk and takes me to the house. When she pulls up in the driveway, my dad comes out of the house on his Hoveround and asks her, "What in the hell did you do to my son?" She looks at him with tears in her eyes and says, "I'm so sorry, sir. I just didn't see him."

My dad immediately takes me to the hospital, and after getting checked out, I'm informed that I have some serious problems. The impact cracked the bone in my neck, and I have two herniated disks in my cervical. It also ruptured a disk in my lower back, and I have two herniated disks in my lumbar.

Two days later our family attorney advises me to see another doctor, and from there I'm sent to an advanced orthopedic surgeon. Now that it's been two days since the accident, the pain is really starting to set in, and I'm not a happy camper wearing this freaking neck brace. A couple of days later, Mrs. White, who is an elder from church, comes to visit me, and the first thing that she says is "You know that the devil is trying to kill you, don't you?"

"Yes, ma'am," I reply, "I'm fully aware of that, but the Lord won't let him have me." I must admit that I'm somewhat surprised to hear her say that, but then again she knows that Satan is angry with me because I'm trying to do the Lord's work.

There is a positive side to this accident, and it's that I now know where my financial resources are going to come from. According to my attorney, I now have a six-figure settlement that's going to be coming my way. That'll be more than enough to get me out of debt with child support and to reunite me with my kids. I'll also have enough to record, produce, and publish my music and book. The Lord works in mysterious ways.

After being laid up in bed and going back and forth to the doctor for weeks, I'm finally able to move around a little bit more. When I get to Ms. Tangy's crib, she says that she has some bad news for me. She's not pregnant, and the reason that she has missed her cycle and gained excessive weight over the past few months is because of some other medical condition.

Wow, I'm sad and happy. I'm sad that she's not having my baby, then on the other hand, I'm happy that she's not having my baby. I already have a baby, and her name is K. She may be nine years old, but she's still my baby girl and no one can ever change that. I also have an eleven-year-old son named A, whom I love just as well. T is my firstborn, and he will always have a special place in my heart. When I get straight, I will most definitely prepare a place for them all.

Since Ms. Tangy is not pregnant, we've been seeing a lot less of each other. I actually miss her daughters more than I miss her, especially Snoopy and AD; they're absolutely my favorites. I'm also very concerned about Mirror because there has been an ongoing series of unsettling events with her dad.

Just a couple of days ago when she returned from a weekend visit with her dad, she complained about irritation in her private area. She was actually terrified about taking a bath, and when Ms. Tangy took her to the doctor, she was very sensitive and red in that area. God forbid if her dad is touching her inappropriately. Who does that to a child, especially his own child at that? Even if he didn't do it, he's still responsible if someone else did.

He's fully aware that I've been seeing Ms. Tangy for the past seven months, and that fact is eating him up inside. His own daughter Mirror has told him several times that she loves me, and I'm sure that bothers him as well. If this is his sick way of retaliation, the Lord is going to punish him severely, because "Revenge is mine," said the Lord.

Due to the seriousness of the situation, the Department of Family and Children Services has launched an investigation. If it were my child, there is no way in hell that I would allow him to pick her up again for the weekend. However, Ms. Tangy is on probation, so maybe she's afraid of getting arrested for not following the court order concerning his visitation rights.

Two weeks later, I'm at Ms. Tangy's crib, chilling as Mirror returns from another visit with her dad, and she's complaining about her private area again. This time she reluctantly tells us something that's very disturbing, and I can tell that she knows right from wrong because she seems to be very embarrassed to talk about it. She told us that her dad makes her get in the shower with him, and now I'm totally frenetic.

I feel so sorry for her, and it literally makes me cry inside and out. This has got to stop. Who does that? How can this guy have the audacity to call himself a Jehovah's Witness, when in all reality, he's nothing short of a freaking monster that preys on his own three-year-old daughter? I want to hurt him so bad that I can almost taste his blood on my hands, and that's keeping it real. Later when I tell my dad about it, he cries as well because he loves that little girl just as much as or more than I do.

A few days later, Ms. Tangy calls me and says that her probation officer wants her to go to the office to take a drug test. She says that she's dirty and she wants my advice as to what she should do. I advise her to go to the emergency room and play sick. That will buy her some time to get clean and also give her the paperwork that's excusable. Today is Friday, so she'll at least have until Monday to report. I know that it'll work, because I did the same thing years ago.

Unfortunately, she doesn't take my advice, because she doesn't want to spend hours in the emergency room. I would rather spend hours in the emergency room than to spend days in jail any day. As a kid, my mom used to tell me all the time that a hard head will make a soft behind, so I have a feeling that Ms. Tangy is going to regret being hardheaded.

With all the drama that's going on with her baby's daddy, sure enough, when Monday rolls around, things go from bad to worse. Even though she passed the drug test, they arrest her for not reporting on Friday. She calls me and asks me to pick up girls and take them to one of her girlfriends' home. Dang, I hate that; now Mirror has no protection at all until Ms. Tangy gets released, and only God knows when that will be.

After thirty days, her baby's daddy hires an attorney and gets her released. Two weeks after that, she goes to the courthouse and marries the guy. "Are you freaking kidding me?" I ask her. Her kids, her friends, and every one that knows her are completely blown away. After all the dirt that she told me and all the things that I've witnessed myself, you mean to tell me that she married that monster?

We cry together as she tells me the reason behind her decision. She says that he was trying to take her daughter away from her, and the only way that she knew how to stop him was to marry him. She says, "Sergio, this is the only way that I can protect my daughter, because now he can't take her for the weekend anymore."

She claims to be still in love with me, and he's fully aware of that fact. I played a big part in the reason why he wanted to marry her so fast, and now he has her. I must admit that I'm hurt by this because I'm still in love with her as well. Snoopy and AD try their best to comfort me, because early in the relationship, they made me promise to them that I wouldn't hurt their mother.

As I leave her presence, I'm reminded by the Lord that I already have the greatest love of all, which is the love of Jesus Christ. God knows what he's doing, and apparently she is not the one for me. I know that as well; it's just that I'd gotten myself attached to her and her kids. God wants me to focus on him and to keep him first. At the end of the day, I refuse to let anyone or anything steal my joy.

As the weeks go by, Ms. Tangy is still calling me and telling me how much she loves me, and occasionally she finds her way back to me. Two months after her marriage to the monster, she finds out that she's four months pregnant, and this time she has the doctor's report to prove it. It doesn't take a rocket scientist to figure out that I am the father, so here we go again with this baby drama.

Her husband knows that the baby is not his, and now he feels like an idiot for marrying her so soon. His family and his friends have told him that there is no way that the baby can be his. He's pissed, and so am I, knowing that he's lying next to my baby every night even though she's still in the womb.

Ms. Tangy and I meet up with each other to discuss the situation, and I tell her that it'll be a cold day in hell before I let him be a part of my baby's life. If he did all the things to his own daughter that he's being accused of, then I would hate to think of what he would do to mine. In any event or manner, I can't allow that to happen, so I take it to the Lord in prayer.

Three weeks later she calls me and tells me that she lost the baby. I don't believe her. I think that she aborted my baby just to avoid the embarrassment of having my child while being married to someone else. I have no choice but to let it go because apparently it's the Lord's will. At this point I can finally wash my hands of her and her husband, so I wish her well.

Three months later it's time for me to move on and find myself another companion, so I decide to try online dating for the first time. I have been diligently studying the Word day in and day out for months, and now I feel like it's time for me to meet someone new.

After posting my profile online, the number of responses that I'm getting is overwhelming. I can't keep up with all these women, and at times I really don't know whom I'm talking to. Out of all the women on the site, there's one that I'm truly interested in. Her name is Miranda, and she's in Stone Mountain, Georgia.

I can't put my finger on what it is about her that I like so much; it's as if my spirit is just drawn to her. She's been playing very hard to get, and I like that about her. So perhaps when I make it back to Atlanta, just maybe I can convince her to go out with me.

In the meantime I have two prospects here in Florida, Yolanda and Rena. As the weeks go by, I've been dating the both of them. I shared my ideas with Yolanda about writing a book and recording a gospel CD, and she is very supportive. She actually spent a thousand dollars on a brand-new laptop computer and gave it to me. I tried my best to talk her out of it, but she said that God told her to buy it for me, so how can I not accept it?

I guess that's my confirmation that he wants me to write the book, so I'm going to start writing it again. God is so amazing, and he's providing the resources that I need to fulfill my purpose. Who would've ever thought that this girl would just go out and do this for me? He's obviously using her as a vessel to help me.

I'm still questioning Yolanda's motive because no one has ever done something like this for me before. I make sure that she knows that I'm moving back to Atlanta as soon as my settlement comes, because I don't want her to feel that I took advantage of her. She says, "Sergio, I'm going to tell this once again. God told me to buy you that computer, and I only did what I was told to do. Don't worry." She says, "I did it with no strings attached."

Rena, on the other hand, has a purpose as well; she just so happens to have a beautiful voice. She sings in the choir at her church, and she has the Holy Ghost inside her. I will definitely be using her gift when I get ready to record my CD. Man, I'm telling you, the Lord is putting everything in place for me.

I'm no longer dibbling and dabbling in the Word; I've made it a part of my life. I've been constantly chiseling my way to Jesus and I have finally broken through, so now I'm out. I'm out of depth, I'm out of fear, I'm out of pain, and I'm out of sin. Glory be to God I'm born again, and for me there is no death. I've reached the pinnacle of eternal life.

CPSIA information can be obtained at www.ICGtesting.com
Printed in the USA
LVOW122043200912

299616LV00001B/5/P